The Law

Frédéric Bastiat

Also included:

"The Broken Window" & "The Candlemakers' Petition"

FEE.org

FEE's mission is to inspire, educate, and connect future leaders with the economic, ethical, and legal principles of a free society.

Find us online at:
FEE.org
Facebook.com/FEEonline
Twitter.com/FEEonline (@feeonline)

Foundation for Economic Education
1819 Peachtree Road NE, Suite 300
Atlanta, Georgia 30309

Telephone: (404) 554-9980

ISBN: 978-157246-553-4

First Edition: 1950
Second Edition: 1998
Third Edition: 2004
Fourth Edition: 2014
Fifth Edition: 2019

Cover design by Tim Webster

Contents

The Law

Foreword

Walter E. Williams

I must have been forty years old before reading Frédéric Bastiat's classic *The Law*. An anonymous person, to whom I shall eternally be in debt, mailed me an unsolicited copy. After reading the book I was convinced that a liberal-arts education without an encounter with Bastiat is incomplete. Reading Bastiat made me keenly aware of all the time wasted, along with the frustrations of going down one blind alley after another, organizing my philosophy of life. *The Law* did not produce a philosophical conversion for me as much as it created order in my thinking about liberty and just human conduct.

Many philosophers have made important contributions to the discourse on liberty, Bastiat among them. But Bastiat's greatest contribution is that he took the discourse out of the ivory tower and made ideas on liberty so clear that even the unlettered can understand them and statists cannot obfuscate them. Clarity is crucial to persuading our fellowman of the moral superiority of personal liberty.

Like others, Bastiat recognized that the greatest single threat to liberty is government. Notice the clarity he employs to help us identify and understand evil government acts such as legalized plunder. Bastiat

Walter E. Williams is the John M. Olin Distinguished Professor of Economics at George Mason University, Fairfax, Virginia.

says, "See if the law takes from some persons what belongs to them, and gives it to other persons to whom it does not belong. See if the law benefits one citizen at the expense of another by doing what the citizen himself cannot do without committing a crime." With such an accurate description of legalized plunder, we cannot deny the conclusion that most government activities, including ours, are legalized plunder, or for the sake of modernity, legalized theft.

Frédéric Bastiat could have easily been a fellow traveler of the signers of our Declaration of Independence. The signers' vision of liberty and the proper role of government was captured in the immortal words "We hold these truths to be self-evident, that all men are created equal, that they are endowed by their Creator with certain Unalienable Rights, that among these are Life, Liberty, and the pursuit of Happiness. That to secure these rights, governments are instituted among Men…." Bastiat echoes the identical vision, saying, "Life, faculties, production—in other words individuality, liberty, property—that is man. And in spite of the cunning of artful political leaders, these three gifts from God precede all human legislation, and are superior to it." Bastiat gave the same rationale for government as did our Founders, saying, "Life, liberty, and property do not exist because men have made laws. On the contrary, it was the fact that life, liberty, and property existed beforehand that caused men to make laws in the first place." No finer statements of natural or God-given rights have been made than those found in our Declaration of Independence and *The Law.*

Bastiat pinned his hopes for liberty on the United States saying, "…look at the United States. There is no country in the world where the law is kept more within its proper domain: the protection of every person's liberty and property. As a consequence of this, there appears to be no country in the world where the social order rests on a firmer foundation." Writing in 1850, Bastiat noted two areas where the United States fell short: "Slavery is a violation, by law, of liberty. The protective tariff is a violation, by law, of property."

If Bastiat were alive today, he would be disappointed with our failure to keep the law within its proper domain. Over the course of a century and a half, we have created more than 50,000 laws. Most of them permit the state to initiate violence against those who have not initiated violence against others. These laws range from anti-smoking laws for private establishments and Social Security "contributions" to licensure laws and minimum wage laws. In each case, the person who resolutely demands and defends his God-given right to be left alone can ultimately suffer death at the hands of our government.*

Bastiat explains the call for laws that restrict peaceable, voluntary exchange and punish the desire to be left alone by saying that social ists want to play God. Socialists look upon people as raw material to be formed into social combinations. To them—the elite—"the relationship between persons and the legislator appears to be the same as the relationship between the clay and the potter." And for people who have this vision, Bastiat displays the only anger I find in *The Law* when he lashes out at do-gooders and would-be rulers of mankind, "Ah, you miserable creatures! You who think that you are so great! You who judge humanity to be so small! You who wish to reform everything! Why don't you reform yourselves? That task would be sufficient enough."

Bastiat was an optimist who thought that eloquent arguments in defense of liberty might save the day; but history is not on his side. Mankind's history is one of systematic, arbitrary abuse and control by the elite acting privately, through the church, but mostly through government. It is a tragic history where hundreds of millions of unfortunate souls have been slaughtered, mostly by their own governments. A historian writing 200 or 300 years from now might view the liberties that existed for a tiny portion of mankind's population, mostly in the

---

*Death is not the stated penalty for disobedience; however, death can occur if the person refuses to submit to government sanctions for his disobedience.

Western world, for only a tiny portion of its history, the last century or two, as a historical curiosity that defies explanation. That historian might also observe that the curiosity was only a temporary phenomenon and mankind reverted back to the traditional state of affairs—arbitrary control and abuse.

Hopefully, history will prove that pessimistic assessment false. The worldwide collapse of the respectability of the ideas of socialism and communism suggests that there is a glimmer of hope. Another hopeful sign is the technological innovations that make it more difficult for government to gain information on its citizens and control them. Innovations such as information access, communication, and electronic monetary transactions will make government attempts at control more costly and less probable. These technological innovations will increasingly make it possible for world citizens to communicate and exchange with one another without government knowledge, sanction, or permission.

The collapse of communism and technological innovations, accompanied by robust free-market organizations promoting Bastiat's ideas, are the most optimistic things I can say about the future of liberty in the United States. Americans share an awesome burden and moral responsibility. If liberty dies in the United States, it is destined to die everywhere. A greater familiarity with Bastiat's clear ideas about liberty would be an important step in rekindling respect and love, and allowing the resuscitation of the spirit of liberty among our fellow Americans.

The Law

The law perverted! And the police powers of the state perverted along with it! The law, I say, not only turned from its proper purpose but made to follow an entirely contrary purpose! The law become the weapon of every kind of greed! Instead of checking crime, the law itself guilty of the evils it is supposed to punish!

If this is true, it is a serious fact, and moral duty requires me to call the attention of my fellow-citizens to it.

Life Is a Gift from God

We hold from God the gift which includes all others. This gift is life—physical, intellectual, and moral life.

But life cannot maintain itself alone. The Creator of life has entrusted us with the responsibility of preserving, developing, and perfecting it. In order that we may accomplish this, He has provided us with a collection of marvelous faculties. And He has put us in the midst of a variety of natural resources. By the application of our faculties to these natural resources we convert them into products, and use them. This process is necessary in order that life may run its appointed course.

Life, faculties, production—in other words, individuality, liberty, property—this is man. And in spite of the cunning of artful political leaders, these three gifts from God precede all human legislation, and are superior to it. Life, liberty, and property do not exist because men have made laws. On the contrary, it was the fact that life, liberty, and property existed beforehand that caused men to make laws in the first place.

Law and Government Properly Defined

What, then, is law? It is the collective organization of the individual right to lawful defense.

Each of us has a natural right—from God—to defend his person, his liberty, and his property. These are the three basic requirements of life, and the preservation of any one of them is completely dependent upon the preservation of the other two. For what are our faculties but the extension of our individuality? And what is property but an extension of our faculties?

If every person has the right to defend—even by force—his person, his liberty, and his property, then it follows that a group of men have the right to organize and support a common force to protect these rights constantly. Thus the principle of collective right—its reason for existing, its lawfulness—is based on individual right. And the common force that protects this collective right cannot logically have any other purpose or any other mission than that for which it acts as a substitute. Thus, since an individual cannot lawfully use force against the person, liberty, or property of another individual, then the common force—for the same reason—cannot lawfully be used to destroy the person, liberty, or property of individuals or groups.

Such a perversion of force would be, in both cases, contrary to our premise. Force has been given to us to defend our own individual rights. Who will dare to say that force has been given to us to destroy the equal rights of our brothers? Since no individual acting separately can lawfully use force to destroy the rights of others, does it not logically follow that the same principle also applies to the common force that is nothing more than the organized combination of the individual forces?

If this is true, then nothing can be more evident than this: The law is the organization of the natural right of lawful defense. It is the substitution of a common force for individual forces. And this common force is to do only what the individual forces have a natural and lawful right to do: to protect persons, liberties, and properties; to maintain the right of each, and to cause *justice* to reign over us all.

A Just and Enduring Government

If a nation were founded on this basis, it seems to me that order would prevail among the people, in thought as well as in deed. It seems to me that such a nation would have the most simple, easy to accept, economical, limited, non-oppressive, just, and enduring government imaginable—whatever its political form might be.

Under such an administration, everyone would understand that he possessed all the privileges as well as all the responsibilities of his existence. No one would have any argument with government, provided that his person was respected, his labor was free, and the fruits of his labor were protected against all unjust attack. When successful, we would not have to thank the state for our success. And, conversely, when unsuccessful, we would no more think of blaming the state for our misfortune than would the farmers blame the state because of hail or frost. The state would be felt only by the invaluable blessings of safety provided by this concept of government.

It can be further stated that, thanks to the non-intervention of the state in private affairs, our wants and their satisfactions would develop themselves in a logical manner. We would not see poor families seeking literary instruction before they have bread. We would not see cities populated at the expense of rural districts, nor rural districts at the expense of cities. We would not see the great displacements of capital, labor, and population that are caused by legislative decisions.

The sources of our existence are made uncertain and precarious by these state-created displacements. And, furthermore, these acts burden the government with increased responsibilities.

Complete Perversion of the Law

But, unfortunately, law by no means confines itself to its proper functions. And when it has exceeded its proper functions, it has not done so merely in some inconsequential and debatable matters. The law has gone further than this; it has acted in direct opposition to its own purpose. The law has been used to destroy its own objective: It has been applied to annihilating the justice that it was supposed to maintain; to limiting and destroying rights which its real purpose was to respect. The law has placed the collective force at the disposal of the unscrupulous who wish, without risk, to exploit the person, liberty, and property of others. It has converted plunder into a right, in order to protect plunder. And it has converted lawful defense into a crime, in order to punish lawful defense.

How has this perversion of the law been accomplished? And what have been the results?

The law has been perverted by the influence of two entirely different causes: stupid greed and false philanthropy. Let us speak of the first.

A Fatal Tendency of Mankind

Self-preservation and self-development are common aspirations among all people. And if everyone enjoyed the unrestricted use of his faculties and the free disposition of the fruits of his labor, social progress would be ceaseless, uninterrupted, and unfailing.

But there is also another tendency that is common among people. When they can, they wish to live and prosper at the expense of others. This is no rash accusation. Nor does it come from a gloomy and uncharitable spirit. The annals of history bear witness to the truth of it: the incessant wars, mass migrations, religious persecutions, universal slavery, dishonesty in commerce, and monopolies. This fatal desire has its origin in the very nature of man—in that primitive, universal, and insuppressible instinct that impels him to satisfy his desires with the least possible pain.

Property and Plunder

Man can live and satisfy his wants only by ceaseless labor; by the ceaseless application of his faculties to natural resources. This process is the origin of property.

But it is also true that a man may live and satisfy his wants by seizing and consuming the products of the labor of others. This process is the origin of plunder.

Now since man is naturally inclined to avoid pain—and since labor is pain in itself—it follows that men will resort to plunder whenever plunder is easier than work. History shows this quite clearly. And under these conditions, neither religion nor morality can stop it.

When, then, does plunder stop? It stops when it becomes more painful and more dangerous than labor.

It is evident, then, that the proper purpose of law is to use the power of its collective force to stop this fatal tendency to plunder instead of to work. All the measures of the law should protect property and punish plunder.

But, generally, the law is made by one man or one class of men. And since law cannot operate without the sanction and support of a dominating force, this force must be entrusted to those who make the laws.

This fact, combined with the fatal tendency that exists in the heart of man to satisfy his wants with the least possible effort, explains the almost universal perversion of the law. Thus it is easy to understand how law, instead of checking injustice, becomes the invincible weapon of injustice. It is easy to understand why the law is used by the legislator to destroy in varying degrees among the rest of the people, their personal independence by slavery, their liberty by oppression, and their property by plunder. This is done for the benefit of the person who makes the law, and in proportion to the power that he holds.

Victims of Lawful Plunder

Men naturally rebel against the injustice of which they are victims. Thus, when plunder is organized by law for the profit of those who make the law, all the plundered classes try somehow to enter—by peaceful or revolutionary means—into the making of laws.

According to their degree of enlightenment, these plundered classes may propose one of two entirely different purposes when they attempt to attain political power: Either they may wish to stop lawful plunder, or they may wish to share in it.

Woe to the nation when this latter purpose prevails among the mass victims of lawful plunder when they, in turn, seize the power to make laws!

Until that happens, the few practice lawful plunder upon the many, a common practice where the right to participate in the making of law is limited to a few persons. But then, participation in the making of law becomes universal. And then, men seek to balance their conflicting interests by universal plunder. Instead of rooting out the injustices found in society, they make these injustices general.

As soon as the plundered classes gain political power, they establish a system of reprisals against other classes. They do not abolish legal plunder. (This objective would demand more enlightenment than they possess.) Instead, they emulate their evil predecessors by participating in this legal plunder, even though it is against their own interests.

It is as if it were necessary, before a reign of justice appears, for everyone to suffer a cruel retribution—some for their evilness, and some for their lack of understanding.

The Results of Legal Plunder

It is impossible to introduce into society a greater change and a greater evil than this: the conversion of the law into an instrument of plunder.

What are the consequences of such a perversion? It would require volumes to describe them all. Thus we must content ourselves with pointing out the most striking.

In the first place, it erases from everyone's conscience the distinction between justice and injustice.

No society can exist unless the laws are respected to a certain degree. The safest way to make laws respected is to make them respectable. When law and morality contradict each other, the citizen has the cruel alternative of either losing his moral sense or losing his respect for the law. These two evils are of equal consequence, and it would be difficult for a person to choose between them.

The nature of law is to maintain justice. This is so much the case that, in the minds of the people, law and justice are one and the same thing. There is in all of us a strong disposition to believe that anything lawful is also legitimate. This belief is so widespread that many persons have erroneously held that things are "just" because law makes them so. Thus, in order to make plunder appear just and sacred to many consciences, it is only necessary for the law to decree and sanction it. Slavery, restrictions, and monopoly find defenders not only among those who profit from them but also among those who suffer from them.

If you suggest a doubt as to the morality of these institutions, it is boldly said that "You are a dangerous innovator, a utopian, a theorist, a subversive; you would shatter the foundation upon which society rests."

If you lecture upon morality or upon political science, there will be found official organizations petitioning the government in this vein of thought: "That science no longer be taught exclusively from the point of view of free trade (of liberty, of property, and of justice) as has been the case until now, but also, in the future, science is to be especially taught from the viewpoint of the facts and laws that regulate French industry (facts and laws which are contrary to liberty, to property, and to justice). That, in government-endowed teaching positions, the professor rigorously refrain from endangering in the slightest degree the respect due to the laws now in force."[*]

Thus, if there exists a law which sanctions slavery or monopoly, oppression or robbery, in any form whatever, it must not ever be mentioned. For how can it be mentioned without damaging the respect which it inspires? Still further, morality and political economy must be taught from the point of view of this law; from the supposition that it must be a just law merely because it is a law.

Universal Suffrage?

Another effect of this tragic perversion of the law is that it gives an exaggerated importance to political passions and conflicts, and to politics in general.

I could prove this assertion in a thousand ways. But, by way of illustration, I shall limit myself to a subject that has lately occupied the minds of everyone: universal suffrage.

The followers of Rousseau's school of thought—who consider themselves far advanced, but whom I consider twenty centuries behind the times—will not agree with me on this. But universal suffrage—using the word in its strictest sense—is not one of those sacred dogmas which it is a crime to examine or doubt. In fact, serious objections may be made to universal suffrage.

In the first place, the word *universal* conceals a gross fallacy. For example, there are 36 million people in France. Thus, to make the right of suffrage universal, there should be 36 million voters. But the most extended system permits only 9 million people to vote. Three persons

---

[*]General Council of Manufacturers, Agriculture, and Commerce, May 6, 1850.

out of four are excluded. And more than this, they are excluded by the fourth. This fourth person advances the principle of *incapacity* as his reason for excluding the others. Universal suffrage means, then, universal suffrage for those who are capable. But there remains this question of fact: Who is capable? Are minors, females, insane persons, and persons who have committed certain major crimes the only ones to be determined incapable?

A closer examination of the subject shows us the motive which causes the right of suffrage to be based upon the supposition of incapacity. The motive is that the elector or voter does not exercise this right for himself alone, but for everybody.

The most extended elective system and the most restricted elective system are alike in this respect. They differ only in respect to what constitutes incapacity. It is not a difference of principle, but merely a difference of degree.

If, as the republicans of our present-day Greek and Roman schools of thought pretend, the right of suffrage arrives with one's birth, it would be an injustice for adults to prevent women and children from voting. Why are they prevented? Because they are presumed to be incapable. And why is incapacity a motive for exclusion? Because it is not the voter alone who suffers the consequences of his vote; because each vote touches and affects everyone in the entire community; because the people in the community have a right to demand some safeguards concerning the acts upon which their welfare and existence depend.

I know what might be said in answer to this; what the objections might be. But this is not the place to exhaust a controversy of this nature. I wish merely to observe here that this controversy over universal suffrage (as well as most other political questions) which agitates, excites, and overthrows nations, would lose nearly all of its importance if the law had always been what it ought to be.

In fact, if law were restricted to protecting all persons, all liberties, and all properties; if law were nothing more than the organized combination of the individual's right to self-defense; if law were the obstacle, the check, the punisher of all oppression and plunder—is it likely that we citizens would then argue much about the extent of the franchise?

Under these circumstances, is it likely that the extent of the right to vote would endanger that supreme good, the public peace? Is it likely that the excluded classes would refuse to peaceably await the coming of their right to vote? Is it likely that those who had the right to vote would jealously defend their privilege?

If the law were confined to its proper functions, everyone's interest in the law would be the same. Is it not clear that, under these circumstances, those who voted could not inconvenience those who did not vote?

The Fatal Idea of Legal Plunder

But on the other hand, imagine that this fatal principle has been introduced: Under the pretense of organization, regulation, protection, or encouragement, the law takes property from one person and gives it to another; the law takes the wealth of all and gives it to a few—whether farmers, manufacturers, shipowners, artists, or comedians. Under these circumstances, then certainly every class will aspire to grasp the law, and logically so.

The excluded classes will furiously demand their right to vote— and will overthrow society rather than not to obtain it. Even beggars and vagabonds will then prove to you that they also have an incontestable title to vote. They will say to you:

"We cannot buy wine, tobacco, or salt without paying the tax. And a part of the tax that we pay is given by law—in privileges and subsidies—to men who are richer than we are. Others use the law to raise the prices of bread, meat, iron, or cloth. Thus, since everyone else uses the law for his own profit, we also would like to use the law for our own profit. We demand from the law the *right to relief*, which is the poor man's plunder. To obtain this right, we also should be voters and legislators in order that we may organize Beggary on a grand scale for our own class, as you have organized Protection on a grand scale for your class. Now don't tell us beggars that you will act for us, and then toss us, as Mr. Mimerel [textile manufacturer and politician] proposes, 600,000 francs to keep us quiet, like throwing us a bone to gnaw. We have other claims. And anyway, we wish to bargain for ourselves as other classes have bargained for themselves!"

And what can you say to answer that argument!

As long as it is admitted that the law may be diverted from its true purpose—that it may violate property instead of protecting it—then everyone will want to participate in making the law, either to protect himself against plunder or to use it for plunder. Political questions will always be prejudicial, dominant, and all-absorbing. There will be fighting at the door of the Legislative Palace, and the struggle within will be no less furious. To know this, it is hardly necessary to examine what transpires in the French and English legislatures; merely to understand the issue is to know the answer.

Is there any need to offer proof that this odious perversion of the law is a perpetual source of hatred and discord; that it tends to destroy society itself? If such proof is needed, look at the United States [in 1850]. There is no country in the world where the law is kept more within its proper domain: the protection of every person's liberty and property. As a consequence of this, there appears to be no country in the world where the social order rests on a firmer foundation. But even in the United States, there are two issues—and only two—that have always endangered the public peace.

What are these two issues? They are slavery and tariffs. These are the only two issues where, contrary to the general spirit of the republic of the United States, law has assumed the character of a plunderer.

Slavery is a violation, by law, of liberty. The protective tariff is a violation, by law, of property.

It is a most remarkable fact that this double *legal crime*—a sorrowful inheritance from the Old World—should be the only issue which can, and perhaps will, lead to the ruin of the Union. It is indeed impossible to imagine, at the very heart of a society, a more astounding fact than this: *The law has come to be an instrument of injustice.* And if this fact brings terrible consequences to the United States—where the proper purpose of the law has been perverted only in the instances of slavery and tariffs—what must be the consequences in Europe, where the perversion of the law is a principle; a system?

Two Kinds of Plunder

Mr. de Montalembert [politician and writer] adopting the thought contained in a famous proclamation by Mr. Carlier [chief of Paris police], has said: "We must make war against socialism." According to the definition of socialism advanced by Mr. Charles Dupin [political economist], he meant: "We must make war against plunder."

But of what plunder was he speaking? For there are two kinds of plunder: legal and illegal.

I do not think that illegal plunder, such as theft or swindling—which the penal code defines, anticipates, and punishes—can be called socialism. It is not this kind of plunder that systematically threatens the foundations of society. Anyway, the war against this kind of plunder has not waited for the command of these gentlemen. The war against illegal plunder has been fought since the beginning of the world. Long before the Revolution of February 1848—long before the appearance even of socialism itself—France had provided police, judges, gendarmes, prisons, dungeons, and scaffolds for the purpose of fighting illegal plunder. The law itself conducts this war, and it is my wish and opinion that the law should always maintain this attitude toward plunder.

But it does not always do this. Sometimes the law defends plunder and participates in it. Thus the beneficiaries are spared the shame, danger, and scruple which their acts would otherwise involve. Sometimes the law places the whole apparatus of judges, police, prisons, and gendarmes at the service of the plunderers, and treats the victim—when he defends himself—as a criminal. In short, there is a *legal plunder*, and it is of this, no doubt, that Mr. de Montalembert speaks.

This legal plunder may be only an isolated stain among the legislative measures of the people. If so, it is best to wipe it out with a minimum of speeches and denunciations—and in spite of the uproar of the vested interests.

Legal Plunder Defined

But how is this legal plunder to be identified? Quite simply. See if the law takes from some persons what belongs to them, and gives it to other persons to whom it does not belong. See if the law benefits one citizen at the expense of another by doing what the citizen himself cannot do without committing a crime.

Then abolish this law without delay, for it is not only an evil itself, but also it is a fertile source for further evils because it invites reprisals. If such a law—which may be an isolated case—is not abolished immediately, it will spread, multiply, and develop into a system.

The person who profits from this law will complain bitterly, defending his *acquired rights*. He will claim that the state is obligated to protect and encourage his particular industry; that this procedure enriches the state because the protected industry is thus able to spend more and to pay higher wages to the poor workingmen.

Do not listen to this sophistry by vested interests. The acceptance of these arguments will build legal plunder into a whole system. In fact, this has already occurred. The present-day delusion is an attempt to enrich everyone at the expense of everyone else; to make plunder universal under the pretense of organizing it.

Legal Plunder Has Many Names

Now, legal plunder can be committed in an infinite number of ways. Thus we have an infinite number of plans for organizing it: tariffs, protection, benefits, subsidies, encouragements, progressive taxation, public schools, guaranteed jobs, guaranteed profits, minimum wages, a right to relief, a right to the tools of labor, free credit, and so on, and so on. All these plans as a whole—with their common aim of legal plunder—constitute socialism.

Now, since under this definition socialism is a body of doctrine, what attack can be made against it other than a war of doctrine? If you find this socialistic doctrine to be false, absurd, and evil, then refute it. And the more false, the more absurd, and the more evil it is, the easier it will be to refute. Above all, if you wish to be strong, begin by rooting out every particle of socialism that may have crept into your legislation. This will be no light task.

Mr. de Montalembert has been accused of desiring to fight socialism by the use of brute force. He ought to be exonerated from this accusation, for he has plainly said: "The war that we must fight against socialism must be in harmony with law, honor, and justice."

But why does not Mr. de Montalembert see that he has placed himself in a vicious circle? You would use the law to oppose socialism? But it is upon the law that socialism itself relies. Socialists desire to practice *legal* plunder, not *illegal* plunder. Socialists, like all other monopolists, desire to make the law their own weapon. And when once the law is on the side of socialism, how can it be used against socialism? For when plunder is abetted by the law, it does not fear your courts, your gendarmes, and your prisons. Rather, it may call upon them for help.

To prevent this, you would exclude socialism from entering into the making of laws? You would prevent socialists from entering the Legislative Palace? You shall not succeed, I predict, so long as legal plunder continues to be the main business of the legislature. It is illogical—in fact, absurd—to assume otherwise.

The Choice Before Us

This question of legal plunder must be settled once and for all, and there are only three ways to settle it:

1. The few plunder the many.

2. Everybody plunders everybody.

3. Nobody plunders anybody.

We must make our choice among limited plunder, universal plunder, and no plunder. The law can follow only one of these three.

Limited legal plunder: This system prevailed when the right to vote was restricted. One would turn back to this system to prevent the invasion of socialism.

Universal legal plunder: We have been threatened with this system since the franchise was made universal. The newly enfranchised majority has decided to formulate law on the same principle of legal plunder that was used by their predecessors when the vote was limited.

No legal plunder: This is the principle of justice, peace, order, stability, harmony, and logic. Until the day of my death, I shall proclaim this principle with all the force of my lungs (which alas! is all too inadequate).*

And, in all sincerity, can anything more than the absence of plunder be required of the law? Can the law—which necessarily requires the use of force—rationally be used for anything except protecting the rights of everyone? I defy anyone to extend it beyond this purpose without perverting it and, consequently, turning might against right. This is the most fatal and most illogical social perversion that can

---

*Translator's note: At the time this was written, Mr. Bastiat knew that he was dying of tuberculosis. Within a year, he was dead.

possibly be imagined. It must be admitted that the true solution—so long searched for in the area of social relationships—is contained in these simple words: *Law is organized justice.*

Now this must be said: When justice is organized by law—that is, by force—this excludes the idea of using law (force) to organize any human activity whatever, whether it be labor, charity, agriculture, commerce, industry, education, art, or religion. The organizing by law of any one of these would inevitably destroy the essential organization—justice. For truly, how can we imagine force being used against the liberty of citizens without it also being used against justice, and thus acting against its proper purpose?

The Seductive Lure of Socialism

Here I encounter the most popular fallacy of our times. It is not considered sufficient that the law should be just; it must be philanthropic. Nor is it sufficient that the law should guarantee to every citizen the free and inoffensive use of his faculties for physical, intellectual, and moral self-improvement. Instead, it is demanded that the law should directly extend welfare, education, and morality throughout the nation.

This is the seductive lure of socialism. And I repeat again: These two uses of the law are in direct contradiction to each other. We must choose between them. A citizen cannot at the same time be free and not free.

Mr. de Lamartine once wrote to me thusly: "Your doctrine is only the half of my program. You have stopped at liberty; I go on to fraternity." I answered him: "The second half of your program will destroy the first."

In fact, it is impossible for me to separate the word *fraternity* from the word *voluntary*. I cannot possibly understand how fraternity can be *legally* enforced without liberty being *legally* destroyed, and thus justice being *legally* trampled underfoot.

The Roots of Plunder

Legal plunder has two roots: One of them, as I have said before, is in human greed; the other is in false philanthropy.

At this point, I think that I should explain exactly what I mean by the word *plunder*.*

I do not, as is often done, use the word in any vague, uncertain, approximate, or metaphorical sense. I use it in its scientific acceptance—as expressing the idea opposite to that of property [wages, land, money, or whatever]. When a portion of wealth is transferred from the person who owns it—without his consent and without compensation, and whether by force or by fraud—to anyone who does not own it, then I say that property is violated; that an act of plunder is committed.

I say that this act is exactly what the law is supposed to suppress, always and everywhere. When the law itself commits this act that it is supposed to suppress, I say that plunder is still committed, and I add that from the point of view of society and welfare, this aggression against rights is even worse. In this case of legal plunder, however, the person who receives the benefits is not responsible for the act of plundering. The responsibility for this legal plunder rests with the law, the legislator, and society itself. Therein lies the political danger.

It is to be regretted that the word *plunder* is offensive. I have tried in vain to find an inoffensive word, for I would not at any time—especially now—wish to add an irritating word to our dissensions. Thus, whether I am believed or not, I declare that I do not mean to attack the intentions or the morality of anyone. Rather, I am attacking an *idea* which I believe to be false; a *system* which appears to me to be unjust; an injustice so independent of personal intentions that each of us profits from it without wishing to do so, and suffers from it without knowing the cause of the suffering.

---

*Translator's note: The French word used by Mr. Bastiat is *spoliation*.

Three Systems of Plunder

The sincerity of those who advocate protectionism, socialism, and communism is not here questioned. Any writer who would do that must be influenced by a political spirit or a political fear. It is to be pointed out, however, that protectionism, socialism, and communism are basically the same plant in three different stages of its growth. All that can be said is that legal plunder is more visible in communism because it is complete plunder; and in protectionism because the plunder is limited to specific groups and industries.* Thus it follows that, of the three systems, socialism is the vaguest, the most indecisive, and, consequently, the most sincere stage of development.

But sincere or insincere, the intentions of persons are not here under question. In fact, I have already said that legal plunder is based partially on philanthropy, even though it is a false philanthropy.

With this explanation, let us examine the value—the origin and the tendency—of this popular aspiration which claims to accomplish the general welfare by general plunder.

Law Is Force

Since the law organizes justice, the socialists ask why the law should not also organize labor, education, and religion.

Why should not law be used for these purposes? Because it could not organize labor, education, and religion without destroying justice. We must remember that law is force, and that, consequently, the

---

*If the special privilege of government protection against competition—a monopoly—were granted only to one group in France, the iron workers, for instance, this act would so obviously be legal plunder that it could not last for long. It is for this reason that we see all the protected trades combined into a common cause. They even organize themselves in such a manner as to appear to represent all persons who labor. Instinctively, they feel that legal plunder is concealed by generalizing it.

proper functions of the law cannot lawfully extend beyond the proper functions of force.

When law and force keep a person within the bounds of justice, they impose nothing but a mere negation. They oblige him only to abstain from harming others. They violate neither his personality, his liberty, nor his property. They safeguard all of these. They are *defensive*; they defend equally the rights of all.

Law Is a Negative Concept

The harmlessness of the mission performed by law and lawful defense is self-evident; the usefulness is obvious; and the legitimacy cannot be disputed.

As a friend of mine once remarked, this negative concept of law is so true that the statement, *the purpose of the law is to cause justice to reign*, is not a rigorously accurate statement. It ought to be stated that *the purpose of the law is to prevent injustice from reigning*. In fact, it is injustice, instead of justice, that has an existence of its own. Justice is achieved only when injustice is absent.

But when the law, by means of its necessary agent, force, imposes upon men a regulation of labor, a method or a subject of education, a religious faith or creed—then the law is no longer negative; it acts positively upon people. It substitutes the will of the legislator for their own wills; the initiative of the legislator for their own initiatives. When this happens, the people no longer need to discuss, to compare, to plan ahead; the law does all this for them. Intelligence becomes a useless prop for the people; they cease to be men; they lose their personality, their liberty, their property.

Try to imagine a regulation of labor imposed by force that is not a violation of liberty; a transfer of wealth imposed by force that is not a violation of property. If you cannot reconcile these contradictions, then you must conclude that the law cannot organize labor and industry without organizing injustice.

The Politician's Approach

When a politician views society from the seclusion of his office, he is struck by the spectacle of the inequality that he sees. He deplores the deprivations which are the lot of so many of our brothers, deprivations which appear to be even sadder when contrasted with luxury and wealth.

Perhaps the politician should ask himself whether this state of affairs has not been caused by old conquests and lootings, and by more recent legal plunder. Perhaps he should consider this proposition: Since all persons seek well-being and perfection, would not a condition of justice be sufficient to cause the greatest efforts toward progress, and the greatest possible equality that is compatible with individual responsibility? Would not this be in accord with the concept of individual responsibility which God has willed in order that mankind may have the choice between vice and virtue, and the resulting punishment and reward?

But the politician never gives this a thought. His mind turns to organizations, combinations, and arrangements—legal or apparently legal. He attempts to remedy the evil by increasing and perpetuating the very thing that caused the evil in the first place: legal plunder. We have seen that justice is a negative concept. Is there even one of these positive legal actions that does not contain the principle of plunder?

The Law and Charity

You say: "There are persons who have no money," and you turn to the law. But the law is not a breast that fills itself with milk. Nor are the lacteal veins of the law supplied with milk from a source outside the society. Nothing can enter the public treasury for the benefit of one citizen or one class unless other citizens and other classes have been *forced* to send it in. If every person draws from the treasury the amount that he has put in it, it is true that the law then plunders nobody. But this procedure does nothing for the persons who have no money. It does not promote equality of income. The law can be an instrument of equalization only as it takes from some persons and gives to other persons. When the law does this, it is an instrument of plunder.

With this in mind, examine the protective tariffs, subsidies, guaranteed profits, guaranteed jobs, relief and welfare schemes, public education, progressive taxation, free credit, and public works. You will find that they are always based on legal plunder, organized injustice.

The Law and Education

You say: "There are persons who lack education" and you turn to the law. But the law is not, in itself, a torch of learning which shines its light abroad. The law extends over a society where some persons have knowledge and others do not; where some citizens need to learn, and others can teach. In this matter of education, the law has only two alternatives: It can permit this transaction of teaching-and-learning to operate freely and without the use of force, or it can force human wills in this matter by taking from some of them enough to pay the teachers who are appointed by government to instruct others, without charge. But in this second case, the law commits legal plunder by violating liberty and property.

The Law and Morality

You say: "Here are persons who are lacking in morality or religion," and you turn to the law. But law is force. And need I point out what a violent and futile effort it is to use force in the matters of morality and religion?

It would seem that socialists, however self-complacent, could not avoid seeing this monstrous legal plunder that results from such systems and such efforts. But what do the socialists do? They cleverly disguise this legal plunder from others—and even from themselves—under the seductive names of fraternity, unity, organization, and association.

Because we ask so little from the law—only justice—the socialists thereby assume that we reject fraternity, unity, organization, and association. The socialists brand us with the name *individualist*.

But we assure the socialists that we repudiate only *forced* organization, not natural organization. We repudiate the forms of association that are *forced* upon us, not free association. We repudiate *forced* fraternity, not true fraternity. We repudiate the *artificial* unity that does nothing more than deprive persons of individual responsibility. We do not repudiate the natural unity of mankind under Providence.

A Confusion of Terms

Socialism, like the ancient ideas from which it springs, confuses the distinction between government and society. As a result of this, every time we object to a thing being done by government, the socialists conclude that we object to its being done at all.

We disapprove of state education. Then the socialists say that we are opposed to any education. We object to a state religion. Then the socialists say that we want no religion at all. We object to a state-enforced equality. Then they say that we are against equality. And so on, and so on. It is as if the socialists were to accuse us of not wanting persons to eat because we do not want the state to raise grain.

Influence of Socialist Writers

How did politicians ever come to believe this weird idea that the law could be made to produce what it does not contain—the wealth, science, and religion that, in a positive sense, constitute prosperity? Is it due to the influence of our modern writers on public affairs?

Present-day writers—especially those of the socialist school of thought—base their various theories upon one common hypothesis: They divide mankind into two parts. People in general—with the exception of the writer himself—form the first group. The writer, all alone, forms the second and most important group. Surely this is the weirdest and most conceited notion that ever entered a human brain!

In fact, these writers on public affairs begin by supposing that people have within themselves no means of discernment; no motivation to action. The writers assume that people are inert matter, passive particles, motionless atoms, at best a kind of vegetation indifferent to its own manner of existence. They assume that people are susceptible to being shaped—by the will and hand of another person—into an infinite variety of forms, more or less symmetrical, artistic, and perfected.

Moreover, not one of these writers on governmental affairs hesitates to imagine that he himself—under the title of organizer, discoverer, legislator, or founder—is this will and hand, this universal motivating force, this creative power whose sublime mission is to mold these scattered materials—persons—into a society.

These socialist writers look upon people in the same manner that the gardener views his trees. Just as the gardener capriciously shapes the trees into pyramids, parasols, cubes, vases, fans, and other forms, just so does the socialist writer whimsically shape human beings into groups, series, centers, sub-centers, honeycombs, labor corps, and other variations. And just as the gardener needs axes, pruning hooks, saws, and shears to shape his trees, just so does the socialist writer need the force that he can find only in law to shape human beings. For this purpose, he devises tariff laws, tax laws, relief laws, and school laws.

Socialists Want to Play God

Socialists look upon people as raw material to be formed into social combinations. This is so true that, if by chance, the socialists have any doubts about the success of these combinations, they will demand that a small portion of mankind be set aside *to experiment upon.* The popular idea of *trying all systems* is well known. And one socialist leader has been known seriously to demand that the Constituent

Assembly give him a small district with all its inhabitants, to try his experiments upon.

In the same manner, an inventor makes a model before he constructs the full-sized machine; the chemist wastes some chemicals—the farmer wastes some seeds and land—to try out an idea.

But what a difference there is between the gardener and his trees, between the inventor and his machine, between the chemist and his elements, between the farmer and his seeds! And in all sincerity, the socialist thinks that there is the same difference between him and mankind!

It is no wonder that the writers of the nineteenth century look upon society as an artificial creation of the legislator's genius. This idea—the fruit of classical education—has taken possession of all the intellectuals and famous writers of our country. To these intellectuals and writers, the relationship between persons and the legislator appears to be the same as the relationship between the clay and the potter.

Moreover, even where they have consented to recognize a principle of action in the heart of man—and a principle of discernment in man's intellect—they have considered these gifts from God to be fatal gifts. They have thought that persons, under the impulse of these two gifts, would fatally tend to ruin themselves. They assume that if the legislators left persons free to follow their own inclinations, they would arrive at atheism instead of religion, ignorance instead of knowledge, poverty instead of production and exchange.

Socialists Despise Mankind

According to these writers, it is indeed fortunate that Heaven has bestowed upon certain men—governors and legislators—the exact opposite inclinations, not only for their own sake but also for the sake of the rest of the world! While mankind tends toward evil, the legislators yearn for good; while mankind advances toward darkness, the legislators aspire for enlightenment; while mankind is drawn toward vice, the legislators are attracted toward virtue. Since they have decided that this is the true state of affairs, they then demand the use of force in order to substitute their own inclinations for those of the human race.

Open at random any book on philosophy, politics, or history, and you will probably see how deeply rooted in our country is this idea—the child of classical studies, the mother of socialism. In all of them, you will probably find this idea that mankind is merely inert matter, receiving life, organization, morality, and prosperity from the power of the state. And even worse, it will be stated that mankind tends toward degeneration, and is stopped from this downward course only by the mysterious hand of the legislator. Conventional classical thought everywhere says that behind passive society there is a concealed power called *law* or *legislator* (or called by some other terminology that designates some unnamed person or persons of undisputed influence and authority) which moves, controls, benefits, and improves mankind.

Let us first consider a quotation from Bossuet [tutor to the Dauphin in the Court of Louis XIV]:

> One of the things most strongly impressed (by whom?) upon the minds of the Egyptians was patriotism.... *No one was permitted* to be useless to the state. The law assigned to each one his work, which was handed down from father to son. No one was permitted to have two professions. Nor could a person change from one job to another....But there was one task to which all were *forced* to conform: the study of the laws and of wisdom. Ignorance of religion and of the political regulations of the country *was not excused* under any circumstances. Moreover each occupation *was assigned* (by whom?) to a certain district.... Among the good laws, one of the best was that everyone *was trained* (by whom?) to obey them. As a result of this, Egypt was filled with wonderful inventions,

and nothing was neglected that could make life easy and quiet.

Thus, according to Bossuet, persons derive nothing from themselves. Patriotism, prosperity, inventions, husbandry, science—all of these are given to the people by the operation of the laws, the rulers. All that the people have to do is to bow to leadership.

Defense of Paternal Government

Bossuet carries this idea of the state as the source of all progress even so far as to defend the Egyptians against the charge that they rejected wrestling and music. He said:

> How is that possible? These arts were invented by Trismegistus [who was alleged to have been Chancellor to the Egyptian god Osiris].

And again among the Persians, Bossuet claims that all comes from above:

> One of the first responsibilities *of the prince* was to encourage agriculture.... Just as there were offices established for the regulation of armies, just so were there offices for the direction of farm work.... The Persian people *were inspired* with an overwhelming respect for royal authority.

And according to Bossuet, the Greek people, although exceedingly intelligent, had no sense of personal responsibility; like dogs and horses, they themselves could not have invented the most simple games:

> The Greeks, naturally intelligent and courageous, *had been early cultivated* by the kings and settlers who had come from Egypt. From these Egyptian rulers, the Greek people had learned bodily exercises, *foot races,* and horse and chariot races. But the best thing that

the Egyptians had taught the Greeks was to become
docile, and to permit themselves to be formed by the
law for the public good.

The Idea of Passive Mankind

It cannot be disputed that these classical theories [advanced by
these latter-day teachers, writers, legislators, economists, and philoso-
phers] held that everything came to the people from a source outside
themselves. As another example, take Fénelon [archbishop, author, and
instructor to the Duke of Burgundy].

He was a witness to the power of Louis XIV. This, plus the fact
that he was nurtured in the classical studies and the admiration of
antiquity, naturally caused Fénelon to accept the idea that mankind
should be passive; that the misfortunes and the prosperity—vices and
virtues—of people are caused by the external influence exercised upon
them by the law and the legislators. Thus, in his *Utopia of Salentum*, he
puts men—with all their interests, faculties, desires, and possessions—
under the absolute discretion of the legislator. Whatever the issue may
be, persons do not decide it for themselves; the prince decides for
them. The prince is depicted as the *soul* of this shapeless mass of people
who form the nation. In the prince resides the thought, the foresight,
all progress, and the principle of all organization. Thus all responsibility
rests with him.

The whole of the tenth book of Fénelon's *Telemachus* proves this.
I refer the reader to it, and content myself with quoting at random
from this celebrated work to which, in every other respect, I am the
first to pay homage.

Socialists Ignore Reason and Facts

With the amazing credulity which is typical of the classicists,
Fénelon ignores the authority of reason and facts when he attributes

the general happiness of the Egyptians, not to their own wisdom but to the wisdom of their kings:

> We could not turn our eyes to either shore without seeing rich towns and country estates most agreeably located; fields, never fallowed, covered with golden crops every year; meadows full of flocks; workers bending under the weight of the fruit which the earth lavished upon its cultivators; shepherds who made the echoes resound with the soft notes from their pipes and flutes. "Happy," said Mentor, "is the people governed by a wise king…."

Later, Mentor desired that I observe the contentment and abundance which covered all Egypt, where twenty-two thousand cities could be counted. He admired the good police regulations in the cities; the justice rendered in favor of the poor *against* the rich; the sound education of the children in obedience, labor, sobriety, and the love of the arts and letters; the exactness with which all religious ceremonies were performed; the unselfishness, the high regard for honor, the faithfulness to men, and the fear of the gods which every father taught his children. He never stopped admiring the prosperity of the country. "Happy," said he, "is the people ruled by a wise king in such a manner."

Socialists Want to Regiment People

Fénelon's idyl on Crete is even more alluring. Mentor is made to say:

> All that you see in this wonderful island results from the laws of Minos. The education which he ordained

for the children makes their bodies strong and robust. From the very beginning, one accustoms the children to a life of frugality and labor, because one assumes that all pleasures of the senses weaken both body and mind. Thus one allows them no pleasure except that of becoming invincible by virtue, and of acquiring glory....Here one punishes three vices that go unpunished among other people: ingratitude, hypocrisy, and greed. There is no need to punish persons for pomp and dissipation, for they are unknown in Crete....No costly furniture, no magnificent clothing, no delicious feasts, no gilded palaces are permitted.

Thus does Mentor prepare his student to mold and to manipulate—doubtless with the best of intentions—the people of Ithaca.

And to convince the student of the wisdom of these ideas, Mentor recites to him the example of Salentum. It is from this sort of philosophy that we receive our first political ideas! We are taught to treat persons much as an instructor in agriculture teaches farmers to prepare and tend the soil.

A Famous Name and a Frightful Idea

Now listen to the great Montesquieu on this same subject:

To maintain the spirit of commerce, it is necessary that all the laws must favor it. These laws, by proportionately dividing up the fortunes as they are made in commerce, should provide every poor citizen with sufficiently easy circumstances to enable him to work like the others. These same laws should put every rich citizen in such lowered circumstances as to force him to work in order to keep or to gain.

Thus the laws are to dispose of all fortunes!

Although real equality is the soul of the state in a democracy, yet this is so difficult to establish that an extreme precision in this matter would not always be desirable. It is sufficient that here be established a census to reduce or fix these differences in wealth within a certain limit. After this is done, it remains for specific laws to equalize inequality by imposing burdens upon the rich and granting relief to the poor.

Here again we find the idea of equalizing fortunes by law, by force.

In Greece, there were two kinds of republics, One, Sparta, was military; the other, Athens, was commercial. In the former, *it was desired* that the citizens be idle; in the latter, love of labor *was encouraged*.

Note the marvelous genius of these legislators: By debasing all established customs—by mixing the usual concepts of all virtues—they knew in advance that the world would admire their wisdom.

Lycurgus gave stability to his city of Sparta by combining petty thievery with the soul of justice; by combining the most complete bondage with the most extreme liberty; by combining the most atrocious beliefs with the greatest moderation. He appeared to deprive his city of all its resources, arts, commerce, money, and defenses. In Sparta, ambition went without the hope of material reward. Natural affection found no outlet because a man was neither son, husband, nor father. Even chastity was no longer considered becoming. *By this road, Lycurgus led Sparta on to greatness and glory.*

This boldness which was to be found in the institutions of Greece has been repeated in the midst of *the degeneracy and corruption of our modern times.* An occasional honest legislator has molded a people in whom integrity appears as natural as courage in the Spartans.

Mr. William Penn, for example, is a true Lycurgus. Even though Mr. Penn had peace as his objective—while Lycurgus had war as his objective—they resemble each other in that their moral prestige over free men allowed them to overcome prejudices, to subdue passions, and to lead their respective peoples into new paths.

The country of Paraguay furnishes us with another example [of a people who, for their own good, are molded by their legislators].*

Now it is true that if one considers the sheer pleasure of commanding to be the greatest joy in life, he contemplates a crime against society; it will, however, always be a noble ideal to govern men in a manner that will make them happier.

Those who desire to establish similar institutions must do as follows: Establish common ownership of property as in the republic of Plato; revere the gods as Plato commanded; prevent foreigners from mingling with the people, in order to preserve the customs; let the state, instead of the citizens, establish commerce. The legislators should supply arts instead of luxuries; they should satisfy needs instead of desires.

Those who are subject to vulgar infatuation may exclaim: "Montesquieu has said this! So it's magnificent! It's sublime!" As for me, I

---

*Translator's note: What was then known as Paraguay was a much larger area than it is today. It was colonized by the Jesuits who settled the Indians into villages, and generally saved them from further brutalities by the avid conquerors.

have the courage of my own opinion. I say: What! You have the nerve to call that fine? It is frightful! It is abominable! These random selections from the writings of Montesquieu show that he considers persons, liberties, property—mankind itself—to be nothing but materials for legislators to exercise their wisdom upon.

Rousseau and Social Democracy

Now let us examine Rousseau on this subject. This writer on public affairs is the supreme authority of the democrats. And although he bases the social structure upon the *will of the people*, he has, to a greater extent than anyone else, completely accepted the theory of the total inertness of mankind in the presence of the legislators:

> If it is true that a great prince is rare, then is it not true that a great legislator is even more rare? The prince has only to follow the pattern that the legislator creates. *The legislator is the mechanic who invents the machine*; the prince is merely the workman who sets it in motion.

And what part do persons play in all this? They are merely the machine that is set in motion. In fact, are they not merely considered to be the raw material of which the machine is made?

Thus the same relationship exists between the legislator and the prince as exists between the agricultural expert and the farmer; and the relationship between the prince and his subjects is the same as that between the farmer and his land. How high above mankind, then, has this writer on public affairs been placed? Rousseau rules over legislators themselves, and teaches them their trade in these imperious terms:

> Would you give stability to the state? Then bring the extremes as closely together as possible. Tolerate neither wealthy persons nor beggars.
>
> If the soil is poor or barren, or the country too

small for its inhabitants, then turn to industry and arts, and trade these products for the foods that you need.

…On a fertile soil—if *you are short* of inhabitants—devote all your attention to agriculture, because this multiplies people; *banish* the arts, because they only serve to depopulate the nation.…

If you have extensive and accessible coast lines, then *cover the sea* with merchant ships; you will have a brilliant but short existence. If your seas wash only inaccessible cliffs, let the people *be barbarous* and eat fish; they will live more quietly—perhaps better—and, most certainly, they will live more happily.

In short, and in addition to the maxims that are common to all, every people has its own particular circumstances. And this fact in itself will cause legislation appropriate to the circumstances.

This is the reason why the Hebrews formerly—and, more recently, the *Arabs*—had religion as their principle objective. The objective of the Athenians was literature; of Carthage and Tyre, commerce; of Rhodes, naval affairs; of Sparta, war; and of Rome, virtue. The author of *The Spirit of Laws* has shown by what art *the legislator should direct his institutions toward each of these objectives*.… But suppose that the legislator mistakes his proper objective, and acts on a principle different from that indicated by the nature of things? Suppose that the selected principle sometimes creates slavery, and sometimes liberty; sometimes wealth, and sometimes population; sometimes peace, and sometimes conquest? This confusion of objective will slowly enfeeble the law and impair the constitution. The state will be subjected to ceaseless agitations until it is destroyed or changed, and invincible nature regains her empire.

But if nature is sufficiently invincible to *regain* its empire, why does not Rousseau admit that it did not need the legislator to *gain* it in the first place? Why does he not see that men, by obeying their own instincts, would turn to farming on fertile soil, and to commerce on an extensive and easily accessible coast, without the interference of a Lycurgus or a Solon or a Rousseau *who might easily be mistaken.*

Be that as it may, Rousseau invests the creators, organizers, directors, legislators, and controllers of society with a terrible responsibility. He is, therefore, most exacting with them:

> He who would dare to undertake the political creation of a people ought to believe that he can, in a manner of speaking, transform human nature; transform each individual—who, by himself, is a solitary and perfect whole—into a mere part of a greater whole from which the individual will henceforth receive his life and being. Thus the person who would undertake the political creation of a people should believe in his ability to alter man's constitution; to strengthen it; to substitute for the physical and independent existence received from nature, an existence which is partial and moral.* In short, the would-be creator of political man must remove man's own forces and endow him with others that are naturally alien to him.

Poor human nature! What would become of a person's dignity if it were entrusted to the followers of Rousseau?

---

*Translator's note: According to Rousseau, the existence of social man is partial in the sense that he is henceforth merely a part of society. Knowing himself as such—and thinking and feeling from the point of view of the whole—he thereby becomes moral.

Legislators Desire to Mold Mankind

Now let us examine Raynal [French historian and philosopher] on this subject of mankind being molded by the legislator:

> The legislator must first consider the climate, the air, and the soil. The resources at *his* disposal determine his duties. He must first consider *his* locality. A population living on maritime shores must have laws designed for navigation.... If it is an inland settlement, the legislator must make his plans according to the nature and fertility of the soil....
>
> It is especially in the distribution of property that the genius of the legislator will be found. As a general rule, when a new colony is established in any country, sufficient land should be given to each man to support his family....
>
> On an uncultivated island that *you* are populating with children, you need do nothing but let the seeds of truth germinate along with the development of reason....
>
> But when *you* resettle a nation with a past into a new country, the skill of the legislator rests in the policy of *permitting the people* to retain no injurious opinions and customs which can possibly be cured and corrected. If *you* desire to prevent these opinions and customs from becoming permanent, you will secure the second generation by a general system of public education for the children. A prince or a legislator should never establish a colony without first arranging to send wise men along to instruct the youth....
>
> In a new colony, ample opportunity is open to the careful legislator who desires *to purify the customs and*

manners of the people. If he has virtue and genius, the
land and the people *at his disposal* will inspire his soul
with a plan for society. A writer can only vaguely trace
the plan in advance because it is necessarily subject to
the instability of all hypotheses; the problem has many
forms, complications, and circumstances that are difficult to foresee and settle in detail.

Raynal's instructions to the legislators on how to manage people
may be compared to a professor of agriculture lecturing his students:
"The climate is the first rule for the farmer. *His* resources determine
his procedure. He must first consider his locality. If his soil is clay, he
must do so and so. If his soil is sand, he must act in another manner.
Every facility is open to the farmer who wishes to clear and improve
his soil. If he is skillful enough, the manure *at his disposal* will suggest to him a plan of operation. A professor can only vaguely trace this
plan in advance because it is necessarily subject to the instability of all
hypotheses; the problem has many forms, complications, and circumstances that are difficult to foresee and settle in detail."

Oh, sublime writers! Please remember sometimes that this clay,
this sand, and this manure which you so arbitrarily dispose of, are men!
They are your equals! They are intelligent and free human beings like
yourselves! As you have, they too have received from God the faculty
to observe, to plan ahead, to think, and to judge for themselves!

A Temporary Dictatorship

Here is the historian Mably on this subject of the law and the
legislator. In the passages preceding the one here quoted, Mably has
supposed the laws, due to a neglect of security, to be worn out. He
continues to address the reader thusly:

Under these circumstances, it is obvious that the
springs of government are slack. *Give them* a new

tension, and the evil will be cured.... Think less of punishing faults, and more of rewarding *that which you need*. In this manner you will restore to *your republic* the vigor of youth. Because free people have been ignorant of this procedure, they have lost their liberty! But if the evil has made such headway that ordinary governmental procedures are unable to cure it, then *resort* to an extraordinary tribunal with considerable powers for a short time. The imagination of the citizens needs to be struck a hard blow.

In this manner, Mably continues through twenty volumes.

Under the influence of teaching like this—which stems from classical education—there came a time when everyone wished to place himself above mankind in order to arrange, organize, and regulate it in his own way.

Socialist Vision of Equality

Next let us examine Condillac on this subject of the legislators and mankind:

My Lord, assume the character of Lycurgus or of Solon. And before you finish reading this essay, amuse yourself by giving laws to some savages in America or Africa. Confine these nomads to fixed dwellings; teach them to tend flocks.... Attempt to develop the social consciousness that nature has planted in them.... Force them to begin to practice the duties of humanity.... Use punishment to cause sensual pleasures to become distasteful to them. Then you will see that every point of your legislation will cause these savages to lose a vice and gain a virtue.

All people have had laws. But few people have been

happy. Why is this so? Because the legislators themselves have almost always been ignorant of the purpose
of society, which is the uniting of families by a common interest.

Impartiality in law consists of two things: the
establishing of equality in wealth and equality in
dignity among the citizens.... As the laws establish
greater equality, they become proportionately more
precarious to every citizen.... When all men are
equal in wealth and dignity—and when the laws
leave no hope of disturbing this equality—how can
men then be agitated by greed, ambition, dissipation,
idleness, sloth, envy, hatred, or jealousy?

What you have learned about the republic of Sparta
should enlighten you on this question. No other state
has ever had laws more in accord with the order of
nature; of equality.

The Error of the Socialist Writers

Actually, it is *not* strange that during the seventeenth and eighteenth centuries the human race was regarded as inert matter, ready
to receive everything—form, face, energy, movement, life—from
a great prince or great legislator or a great genius. These centuries
were nourished on the study of antiquity. And antiquity presents
everywhere—in Egypt, Persia, Greece, Rome—the spectacle of a
few men molding mankind according to their whims, thanks to the
prestige of force and fraud. But this does not prove that this situation
is desirable. It proves only that since men and society are capable of
improvement, it is naturally to be expected that error, ignorance, despotism, slavery, and superstition should be greatest toward the origins
of history. The writers quoted above were not in error when they
found ancient institutions to be such, but they were in error when

they offered them for the admiration and imitation of future genera-
tions. Uncritical and childish conformists, they took for granted the
grandeur, dignity, morality, and happiness of the artificial societies of
the ancient world. They did not understand that knowledge appears
and grows with the passage of time; and that in proportion to this
growth of knowledge, *might* takes the side of *right*, and society regains
possession of itself.

What Is Liberty?

Actually, what is the political struggle that we witness? It is
the instinctive struggle of all people toward liberty. And what is this
liberty, whose very name makes the heart beat faster and shakes the
world? Is it not the union of all liberties—liberty of conscience, of
education, of association, of the press, of travel, of labor, of trade? In
short, is not liberty the freedom of every person to make full use of
his faculties, so long as he does not harm other persons while doing
so? Is not liberty the destruction of all despotism—including, of
course, legal despotism? Finally, is not liberty the restricting of the law
only to its rational sphere of organizing the right of the individual to
lawful self-defense; of punishing injustice?

It must be admitted that the tendency of the human race toward
liberty is largely thwarted, especially in France. This is greatly due to a
fatal desire—learned from the teachings of antiquity—that our writers on public affairs have in common: They desire to set themselves
above mankind in order to arrange, organize, and regulate it according
to their fancy.

Philanthropic Tyranny

While society is struggling toward liberty, these famous men
who put themselves at its head are filled with the spirit of the seventeenth and eighteenth centuries. They think only of subjecting
mankind to the philanthropic tyranny of their own social inventions.

Like Rousseau, they desire to force mankind docilely to bear this yoke of the public welfare that they have dreamed up in their own imaginations.

This was especially true in 1789. No sooner was the old regime destroyed than society was subjected to still other artificial arrangements, always starting from the same point: the omnipotence of the law.

Listen to the ideas of a few of the writers and politicians during that period:

SAINT-JUST: The legislator commands the future. It is for him to *will* the good of mankind. It is for him to make men what *he wills* them to be.

ROBESPIERRE: The function of government is to direct the physical and moral powers of the nation toward the end for which the commonwealth has come into being.

BILLAUD-VARENNES: A people who are to be returned to liberty must be formed anew. A strong force and vigorous action are necessary to destroy old prejudices, to change old customs, to correct depraved affections, to restrict superfluous wants, and to destroy ingrained vices.... Citizens, the inflexible austerity of Lycurgus created the firm foundation of the Spartan republic. The weak and trusting character of Solon plunged Athens into slavery. This parallel embraces the whole science of government.

LE PELLETIER: Considering the extent of human degradation, I am convinced that it is necessary to effect a total regeneration and, if I may so express myself, of creating a new people.

Socialists Want Tyranny

Again, it is claimed that persons are nothing but raw material. It is not for them to *will their own improvement*; they are incapable of it. According to Saint-Just, only the legislator is capable of doing this. Persons are merely to be what the legislator *wills* them to be. According to Robespierre, who copies Rousseau literally, the legislator begins by decreeing the *end for which the commonwealth has come into being*. Once this is determined, the government has only to direct *the physical and moral forces of the nation* toward that end. Meanwhile, the inhabitants of the nation are to remain completely passive. And according to the teachings of Billaud-Varennes, the people should have no prejudices, no affections, and no desires except those authorized by the legislator. He even goes so far as to say that the inflexible austerity of one man is the foundation of a republic.

In cases where the alleged evil is so great that ordinary governmental procedures cannot cure it, Mably recommends a dictatorship to promote virtue: "Resort," he says, "to an extraordinary tribunal with considerable powers for a short time. The imagination of the citizens needs to be struck a hard blow." This doctrine has not been forgotten. Listen to Robespierre:

> The principle of the republican government is virtue, and the means required to establish virtue is terror. In our country we desire to substitute morality for selfishness, honesty for honor, principles for customs, duties for manners, the empire of reason for the tyranny of fashion, contempt of vice for contempt of poverty, pride for insolence, greatness of soul for vanity, love of glory for love of money, good people for good companions, merit for intrigue, genius for wit, truth for glitter, the charm of happiness for the boredom of pleasure, the greatness of man for the littleness of

the great, a generous, strong, happy people for a good-natured, frivolous, degraded people; in short, we desire to substitute all the virtues and miracles of a republic for all the vices and absurdities of a monarchy.

Dictatorial Arrogance

At what a tremendous height above the rest of mankind does Robespierre here place himself! And note the arrogance with which he speaks. He is not content to pray for a great reawakening of the human spirit. Nor does he expect such a result from a well-ordered government. No, he himself will remake mankind, and by means of terror.

This mass of rotten and contradictory statements is extracted from a discourse by Robespierre in which he aims to explain the *principles of morality which ought to guide a revolutionary government.* Note that Robespierre's request for dictatorship is not made merely for the purpose of repelling a foreign invasion or putting down the opposing groups. Rather he wants a dictatorship in order that he may use terror to force upon the country his own principles of morality. He says that this act is only to be a temporary measure preceding a new constitution. But in reality, he desires nothing short of using terror to extinguish from France *selfishness, honor, customs, manners, fashion, vanity, love of money, good companionship, intrigue, wit, sensuousness, and poverty.* Not until he, Robespierre, shall have accomplished these *miracles,* as he so rightly calls them, will he permit the law to reign again.*

---

*At this point in the original French text, Mr. Bastiat pauses and speaks thusly to all do-gooders and would-be rulers of mankind: "Ah, you miserable creatures! You who think that you are so great! You who judge humanity to be so small! You who wish to reform everything! Why don't you reform yourselves? That task would be sufficient enough."

Indirect Despotism and Passive Mankind

Usually, however, these gentlemen—the reformers, the legislators, and the writers on public affairs—do not desire to impose direct despotism upon mankind. Oh no, they are too moderate and philanthropic for such direct action. Instead, they turn to the law for this despotism, this absolutism, this omnipotence. They desire only to make the laws.

To show the prevalence of this queer idea in France, I would need to copy not only the entire works of Mably, Raynal, Rousseau, and Fénelon—plus long extracts from Bossuet and Montesquieu—but also the entire proceedings of the Convention. I shall do no such thing; I merely refer the reader to them.

It is, of course, not at all surprising that this same idea should have greatly appealed to Napoleon. He embraced it ardently and used it with vigor. Like a chemist, Napoleon considered all Europe to be material for his experiments. But in due course, this material reacted against him.

At St. Helena, Napoleon—greatly disillusioned—seemed to recognize some initiative in mankind. Recognizing this, he became less hostile to liberty. Nevertheless, this did not prevent him from leaving this lesson to his son in his will: "To govern is to increase and spread morality, education, and happiness."

After all this, it is hardly necessary to quote the same opinions from Morelly, Babeuf, Owen, Saint-Simon, and Fourier. Here are, however, a few extracts from Louis Blanc's book on the organization of labor: "In our plan, society receives its momentum from power."

Now consider this: The impulse behind this momentum is to be supplied by the *plan* of Louis Blanc; his plan is to be forced upon society; the Society referred to is the human race. Thus the human race is to receive its momentum from Louis Blanc.

Now it will be said that the people are free to accept or to reject this plan. Admittedly, people are free to accept or to reject *advice* from whomever they wish. But this is not the way in which Mr. Louis Blanc understands the matter. He expects that his plan will be legalized, and thus forcibly imposed upon the people by the power of the law:

> In our plan, the state has only to pass labor laws (nothing else?) by means of which industrial progress can and must proceed *in complete liberty.* The state merely places society on an incline (that is all?). Then society will slide down this incline by the mere force of things, and by the natural workings of the *established mechanism.*

But what is this incline that is indicated by Mr. Louis Blanc? Does it not lead to an abyss? (No, it leads to happiness.) If this is true, then why does not society go there of its own choice? (Because society does not know what it wants; it must be propelled.) What is to propel it? (Power.) And who is to supply the impulse for this power? (Why, the inventor of the machine—in this instance, Mr. Louis Blanc.)

The Vicious Circle of Socialism

We shall never escape from this circle: the idea of passive mankind, and the power of the law being used by a great man to propel the people.

Once on this incline, will society enjoy some liberty? (Certainly.) And what is liberty, Mr. Louis Blanc?

> Once and for all, liberty is not only a mere granted right; it is also the power granted to a person to use and to develop his faculties under a reign of justice and under the protection of the law.

> And this is no pointless distinction; its meaning is deep and its consequences are difficult to estimate. For once it is agreed that a person, to be truly free, must have the power to use and develop his faculties, then

it follows that every person has a claim on society for such education as will *permit him* to develop himself. It also follows that every person has a claim on society for tools of production, without which human activity cannot be fully effective. Now by what action can society give to every person the necessary education and the necessary tools of production, if not by the action of the state?

Thus, again, liberty is power. Of what does this power consist? (Of being educated and of being given the tools of production.) Who is to give the education and the tools of production? (Society, *which owes them to everyone*.) By what action is society to give tools of production to those who do not own them? (Why, *by the action of the state*.) And from whom will the state take them?

Let the reader answer that question. Let him also notice the direction in which this is taking us.

The Doctrine of Social Democracy

The strange phenomenon of our times—one which will probably astound our descendants—is the doctrine based on this triple hypothesis: the total inertness of mankind, the omnipotence of the law, and the infallibility of the legislator. These three ideas form the sacred symbol of those who proclaim themselves totally democratic.

The advocates of this doctrine also profess to be *social*. So far as they are democratic, they place unlimited faith in mankind. But so far as they are social, they regard mankind as little better than mud. Let us examine this contrast in greater detail.

What is the attitude of the democrat when political rights are under discussion? How does he regard the people when a legislator is to be chosen? Ah, then it is claimed that the people have an instinctive wisdom; they are gifted with the finest perception; *their will is always right*; the general will *cannot err*; voting cannot be too universal.

When it is time to vote, apparently the voter is not to be asked for any guarantee of his wisdom. His will and capacity to choose wisely are taken for granted. Can the people be mistaken? Are we not living in an age of enlightenment? What! are the people always to be kept on leashes? Have they not won their rights by great effort and sacrifice? Have they not given ample proof of their intelligence and wisdom? Are they not adults? Are they not capable of judging for themselves? Do they not know what is best for themselves? Is there a class or a man who would be so bold as to set himself above the people, and judge and act for them? No, no, the people are and should be *free*. They desire to manage their own affairs, and they shall do so.

But when the legislator is finally elected—ah! then indeed does the tone of his speech undergo a radical change. The people are returned to passiveness, inertness, and unconsciousness; the legislator enters into omnipotence. Now it is for him to initiate, to direct, to propel, and to organize. Mankind has only to submit; the hour of despotism has struck. We now observe this fatal idea: The people who, during the election, were so wise, so moral, and so perfect, now have no tendencies whatever; or if they have any, they are tendencies that lead downward into degradation.

Socialists Fear All Liberties

But ought not the people be given a little liberty?

But Mr. Considérant has assured us that *liberty leads inevitably to monopoly*!

We understand that liberty means competition. But according to Mr. Louis Blanc, *competition is a system that ruins the businessmen and exterminates the people*. It is for this reason that free people are ruined and exterminated in proportion to their degree of freedom. (Possibly Mr. Louis Blanc should observe the results of competition in, for example, Switzerland, Holland, England, and the United States.)

Mr. Louis Blanc also tells us that *competition leads to monopoly*.

And by the same reasoning, he thus informs us that *low prices lead to high prices*; that *competition drives production to destructive activity*; that *competition drains away the sources of purchasing power*; that *competition forces an increase in production while, at the same time, it forces a decrease in consumption.* From this, it follows that free people produce for the sake of not consuming; that liberty means *oppression and madness* among the people; and that Mr. Louis Blanc absolutely must attend to it.

Well, what liberty should the legislators permit people to have? Liberty of conscience? (But if this were permitted, we would see the people taking this opportunity to become atheists.)

Then liberty of education? (But parents would pay professors to teach their children immorality and falsehoods; besides, according to Mr. Thiers, if education were left to national liberty, it would cease to be national, and we would be teaching our children the ideas of the Turks or Hindus; whereas, thanks to this legal despotism over education, our children now have the good fortune to be taught the noble ideas of the Romans.)

Then liberty of labor? (But that would mean competition which, in turn, leaves production unconsumed, ruins businessmen, and exterminates the people.)

Perhaps liberty of trade? (But everyone knows—and the advocates of protective tariffs have proved over and over again—that freedom of trade ruins every person who engages in it, and that it is necessary to suppress freedom of trade in order to prosper.)

Possibly then, liberty of association? (But, according to socialist doctrine, true liberty and voluntary association are in contradiction to each other, and the purpose of the socialists is to suppress liberty of association precisely in order to force people to associate together in true liberty.)

Clearly then, the conscience of the social democrats cannot permit persons to have any liberty because they believe that the nature of mankind tends always toward every kind of degradation and disaster. Thus, of course, the legislators must make plans for the people in order to save them from themselves.

This line of reasoning brings us to a challenging question: If people are as incapable, as immoral, and as ignorant as the politicians indicate, then why is the right of these same people to vote defended with such passionate insistence?

The Government Shepherds and Their Sheep

The claims of these organizers of humanity raise another question which I have often asked them and which, so far as I know, they have never answered: If the natural tendencies of mankind are so bad that it is not safe to permit people to be free, how is it that the tendencies of these organizers are always good? Do not the legislators and their appointed agents also belong to the human race? Or do they believe that they themselves are made of a finer clay than the rest of mankind? The organizers maintain that society, when left undirected, rushes headlong to its inevitable destruction because the instincts of the people are so perverse. The legislators claim to stop this suicidal course and to give it a saner direction. Apparently, then, the legislators and the organizers have received from Heaven an intelligence and virtue that place them beyond and above mankind; if so, let them show their titles to this superiority.

They would be the shepherds over us, their sheep. Certainly such an arrangement presupposes that they are naturally superior to the rest of us. And certainly we are fully justified in demanding from the legislators and organizers proof of this natural superiority.

Socialists Reject Free Choice

Please understand that I do not dispute their right to invent social combinations, to advertise them, to advocate them, and to try them upon themselves, at their own expense and risk. But I do dispute their right to impose these plans upon us by law—by force—and to compel us to pay for them with our taxes.

I do not insist that the supporters of these various social schools of thought—the Proudhonists, the Cabetists, the Fourierists, the Universitarists, and the Protectionists—renounce their various ideas. I insist only that they renounce this one idea that they have in common: They need only to give up the idea of *forcing* us to acquiesce to their groups and series, their socialized projects, their free-credit banks, their Graeco-Roman concept of morality, and their commercial regulations. I ask only that we be permitted to decide upon these plans for ourselves; that we not be forced to accept them, directly or indirectly, if we find them to be contrary to our best interests or repugnant to our consciences.

But these organizers desire access to the tax funds and to the power of the law in order to carry out their plans. In addition to being oppressive and unjust, this desire also implies the fatal supposition that the organizer is infallible and mankind is incompetent. But, again, if persons are incompetent to judge for themselves, then why all this talk about universal suffrage?

This contradiction in ideas is, unfortunately but logically, reflected in events in France. For example, Frenchmen have led all other Europeans in obtaining their rights—or, more accurately, their political demands. Yet this fact has in no respect prevented us from becoming the most governed, the most regulated, the most imposed upon, the most harnessed, and the most exploited people in Europe. France also leads all other nations as the one where revolutions are constantly to be anticipated. And under the circumstances, it is quite natural that this should be the case.

And this will remain the case so long as our politicians continue to accept this idea that has been so well expressed by Mr. Louis Blanc: "Society receives its momentum from power." This will remain the case so long as human beings with feelings continue to remain passive;

so long as they consider themselves incapable of bettering their prosperity and happiness by their own intelligence and their own energy;
so long as they expect everything from the law; in short, so long as
they imagine that their relationship to the state is the same as that of
the sheep to the shepherd.

Enormous Power of Government

As long as these ideas prevail, it is clear that the responsibility of
government is enormous. Good fortune and bad fortune, wealth and
destitution, equality and inequality, virtue and vice—all then depend
upon political administration. It is burdened with everything, it undertakes everything, it does everything; therefore it is responsible for
everything.

If we are fortunate, then government has a claim to our gratitude;
but if we are unfortunate, then government must bear the blame. For
are not our persons and property now at the disposal of government?
Is not the law omnipotent?

In creating a monopoly of education, the government must
answer to the hopes of the fathers of families who have thus been
deprived of their liberty; and if these hopes are shattered, whose fault
is it?

In regulating industry, the government has contracted to make it
prosper; otherwise it is absurd to deprive industry of its liberty. And if
industry now suffers, whose fault is it?

In meddling with the balance of trade by playing with tariffs, the
government thereby contracts to make trade prosper; and if this results
in destruction instead of prosperity, whose fault is it?

In giving the maritime industries protection in exchange for
their liberty, the government undertakes to make them profitable; and
if they become a burden to the taxpayers, whose fault is it?

Thus there is not a grievance in the nation for which the government does not voluntarily make itself responsible. Is it surprising, then, that every failure increases the threat of another revolution in France?

And what remedy is proposed for this? To extend indefinitely the domain of the law; that is, the responsibility of government.

But if the government undertakes to control and to raise wages, and cannot do it; if the government undertakes to care for all who may be in want, and cannot do it; if the government undertakes to support all unemployed workers, and cannot do it; if the government undertakes to lend interest-free money to all borrowers, and cannot do it; if, in these words that we regret to say escaped from the pen of Mr. de Lamartine, "The state considers that its purpose is to enlighten, to develop, to enlarge, to strengthen, to spiritualize, and to sanctify the soul of the people"—and if the government cannot do all of these things, what then? Is it not certain that after every government failure—which, alas! is more than probable—there will be an equally inevitable revolution?

Economics Precedes Politics

[Now let us return to a subject that was briefly discussed in the opening pages of this thesis: the relationship of economics and of politics—political economy.*]

A science of economics must be developed before a science of politics can be logically formulated. Essentially, economics is the science of determining whether the interests of human beings are harmonious or antagonistic. This must be known before a science of politics can be formulated to determine the proper functions of government.

Immediately following the development of a science of economics, and at the very beginning of the formulation of a science of

---

*Translator's note: Mr. Bastiat has devoted three other books and several articles to the development of the ideas contained in the three sentences of the following paragraph.

politics, this all-important question must be answered: What is law? What ought it to be? What is its scope; its limits? Logically, at what point do the just powers of the legislator stop?

I do not hesitate to answer: *Law is the common force organized to act as an obstacle to injustice.* In short, *law is justice.*

Proper Legislative Functions

It is not true that the legislator has absolute power over our persons and property. The existence of persons and property preceded the existence of the legislator, and his function is only to guarantee their safety.

It is not true that the function of law is to regulate our consciences, our ideas, our wills, our education, our opinions, our work, our trade, our talents, or our pleasures. The function of law is to protect the free exercise of these rights, and to prevent any person from interfering with the free exercise of these same rights by any other person.

Since law necessarily requires the support of force, its lawful domain is only in the areas where the use of force is necessary. This is justice.

Every individual has the right to use force for lawful self-defense. It is for this reason that the collective force—which is only the organized combination of the individual forces—may lawfully be used for the same purpose; and it cannot be used legitimately for any other purpose.

Law is solely the organization of the individual right of self defense which existed before law was formalized. Law is justice.

Law and Charity Are Not the Same

The mission of the law is *not* to oppress persons and plunder them of their property, even though the law may be acting in a philanthropic spirit. Its mission is to protect persons and property.

Furthermore, it must not be said that the law may be

philanthropic if, in the process, it refrains from oppressing persons and plundering them of their property; this would be a contradiction. The law cannot avoid having an effect upon persons and property; and if the law acts in any manner except to protect them, its actions then necessarily violate the liberty of persons and their right to own property.

The law is justice—simple and clear, precise and bounded. Every eye can see it, and every mind can grasp it; for justice is measurable, immutable, and unchangeable. Justice is neither more than this nor less than this.

If you exceed this proper limit—if you attempt to make the law religious, fraternal, equalizing, philanthropic, industrial, literary, or artistic—you will then be lost in an uncharted territory, in vagueness and uncertainty, in a forced utopia or, even worse, in a multitude of utopias, each striving to seize the law and impose it upon you. This is true because fraternity and philanthropy, unlike justice, do not have precise limits. Once started, where will you stop? And where will the law stop itself?

The Road to Communism

Mr. de Saint-Cricq would extend his philanthropy only to some of the industrial groups; he would demand that the law *control the consumers to benefit the producers.*

Mr. Considérant would sponsor the cause of the labor groups; he would use the law to secure for them *a guaranteed minimum of clothing, housing, food, and all other necessities of life.*

Mr. Louis Blanc would say—and with reason—that these minimum guarantees are merely the beginning of complete fraternity; he would say that the law should give tools of production and free education to all working people.

Another person would observe that this arrangement would still leave room for inequality; he would claim that the law should give to everyone—even in the most inaccessible hamlet—luxury, literature, and art.

All of these proposals are the road to communism; legislation will then be—in fact, it already is—the battlefield of all kinds of wild fantasies and unbridled greed.

Law Is Justice

Law is justice. In this proposition a simple and enduring government can be conceived. And I defy anyone to say how even the thought of revolution, of insurrection, of the slightest uprising could arise against a government whose organized force was confined only to suppressing injustice.

Under such a regime, there would be the most prosperity—and it would be the most equally distributed. As for the sufferings that are inseparable from humanity, no one would even think of blaming the government for them. This is true because, if the force of government were limited to suppressing injustice, then government would be as innocent of these sufferings as it is now innocent of changes in the temperature.

As proof of this statement, consider this question: Have the people ever been known to rise against the Court of Appeals, or mob a Justice of the Peace, in order to get higher wages, free credit, tools of production, favorable tariffs, or government-created jobs? Everyone knows perfectly well that such matters are not within the jurisdiction of the Court of Appeals or a Justice of the Peace. And if government were limited to its proper functions, everyone would soon learn that these matters are not within the jurisdiction of the law itself.

But make the laws upon the principle of fraternity—proclaim that all good, and all bad, stem from the law; that the law is responsible for all individual misfortunes and all social inequalities—then the door is open to an endless succession of complaints, irritations, troubles, and revolutions.

Justice Means Equal Rights

Law is justice. And it would indeed be strange if law could properly be anything else! Is not justice right? Are not rights equal? By what right does the law force me to conform to the social plans of Mr. Mimerel, Mr. de Melun, Mr. Thiers, or Mr. Louis Blanc? If the law has a moral right to do this, why does it not, then, force these gentlemen to submit to *my plans*? Is it logical to suppose that nature has not given *me* sufficient imagination to dream up a utopia also? Should the law choose one fantasy among many, and put the organized force of government at its service only?

Law is justice. And let it not be said—as it continually is said—that under this concept, the law would be atheistic, individualistic, and heartless; that it would make mankind in its own image. This is an absurd conclusion, worthy only of those worshipers of government who believe that the law *is* mankind.

Nonsense! Do those worshipers of government believe that free persons will cease to act? Does it follow that if we receive no energy from the law, we shall receive no energy at all? Does it follow that if the law is restricted to the function of protecting the free use of our faculties, we will be unable to use our faculties? Suppose that the law does not force us to follow certain forms of religion, or systems of association, or methods of education, or regulations of labor, or regulations of trade, or plans for charity; does it then follow that we shall eagerly plunge into atheism, hermitary, ignorance, misery, and greed? If we are free, does it follow that we shall no longer recognize the power and goodness of God? Does it follow that we shall then cease to associate with each other, to help each other, to love and succor our unfortunate brothers, to study the secrets of nature, and to strive to improve ourselves to the best of our abilities?

Freedom, Dignity, and Progress

Law is justice. And it is under the law of justice—under the reign of right; under the influence of liberty, safety, stability, and responsibility—that every person will attain his real worth and the true dignity of his being. It is only under this law of justice that mankind will achieve—slowly, no doubt, but certainly—God's design for the orderly and peaceful progress of humanity.

It seems to me that this is theoretically right, for whatever the question under discussion—whether religious, philosophical, political, or economic; whether it concerns prosperity, morality, equality, right, justice, progress, responsibility, cooperation, property, labor, trade, capital, wages, taxes, population, finance, or government—at whatever point on the scientific horizon I begin my researches, I invariably reach this one conclusion: The solution to the problems of human relationships is to be found in liberty.

And does not experience prove this? Look at the entire world. Which countries contain the most peaceful, the most moral, and the happiest people? Those people are found in the countries where the law least interferes with private affairs; where government is least felt; where the individual has the greatest scope, and free opinion the greatest influence; where administrative powers are fewest and simplest; where taxes are lightest and most nearly equal, and popular discontent the least excited and the least justifiable; where individuals and groups most actively assume their responsibilities, and, consequently, where the morals of admittedly imperfect human beings are constantly improving; where trade, assemblies, and associations are the least restricted; where labor, capital, and populations suffer the fewest forced displacements; where mankind most nearly follows its own natural inclinations; where the inventions of men are most nearly in harmony with the laws of God; in short, the happiest, most moral, and most peaceful people are those who most nearly follow this principle: Although mankind is not perfect, still, all hope rests upon the free and voluntary actions of persons within the limits of right; law or force is to be used for nothing except the administration of universal justice.

Do Not Claim to Know More than God

This must be said: There are too many "great" men in the world—legislators, organizers, do-gooders, leaders of the people, fathers of nations, and so on, and so on. Too many persons place themselves above mankind; they make a career of organizing it, patronizing it, and ruling it.

Now someone will say: "You yourself are doing this very thing."

True. But it must be admitted that I act in an entirely different sense; if I have joined the ranks of the reformers, it is solely for the purpose of persuading them to leave people alone. I do not look upon people as Vancauson looked upon his automaton. Rather, just as the physiologist accepts the human body as it is, so do I accept people as they are. I desire only to study and admire.

My attitude toward all other persons is well illustrated by this story from a celebrated traveler: He arrived one day in the midst of a tribe of savages, where a child had just been born. A crowd of soothsayers, magicians, and quacks—armed with rings, hooks, and cords—surrounded it. One said: "This child will never smell the perfume of a peace-pipe unless I stretch his nostrils." Another said: "He will never be able to hear unless I draw his ear-lobes down to his shoulders." A third said: "He will never see the sunshine unless I slant his eyes." Another said: "He will never stand upright unless I bend his legs." A fifth said: "He will never learn to think unless I flatten his skull."

"Stop," cried the traveler. "What God does is well done. Do not claim to know more than He. God has given organs to this frail creature; let them develop and grow strong by exercise, use, experience, and liberty."

Let Us Now Try Liberty!

God has given to men all that is necessary for them to accomplish their destinies. He has provided a social form as well as a human form. And these social organs of persons are so constituted that they will develop themselves harmoniously in the clean air of liberty. Away, then, with quacks and organizers! Away with their rings, chains, hooks, and pincers! Away with their artificial systems! Away with the whims of governmental administrators, their socialized projects, their centralization, their tariffs, their government schools, their state religions, their free credit, their bank monopolies, their regulations, their restrictions, their equalization by taxation, and their pious moralizations!

And now that the legislators and do-gooders have so futilely inflicted so many systems upon society, may they finally end where they should have begun: May they reject all systems, and try liberty; for liberty is an acknowledgment of faith in God and His works.

The Book
and the Author

When a reviewer wishes to give special recognition to a book, he predicts that it will still be read "a hundred years from now." *The Law*, first published as a pamphlet in June 1850, is already more than 150 years old. And because its truths are eternal, it will still be read when another century has passed.

Frédéric Bastiat (1801–1850) was a French economist, statesman, and author. He did most of his writing during the years just before— and immediately following—the Revolution of February 1848. This was a period when France was rapidly turning to complete socialism. As a Deputy to the Legislative Assembly, Mr. Bastiat was studying and explaining each socialist fallacy as it appeared. And he explained how socialism must inevitably degenerate into communism. But most of his countrymen chose to ignore his logic.

The Law is here presented again because the same situation exists in America today as in the France of 1848. The same socialist-communist ideas and plans that were then adopted in France are now sweeping America. The explanations and arguments then advanced by Mr. Bastiat are—word for word—equally valid today. His ideas deserve a serious hearing.

The Translation

Leonard E. Read (1898–1983) is responsible for the rediscovery of Bastiat's classic essay *The Law*. A few years after Mr. Read started the Foundation for Economic Education (FEE), he had the book retranslated from the original French into modern colloquial English. He chose Dean Russell, then a member of the Foundation staff, as the new translator.

A nineteenth-century translation of *The Law*, made in 1853 in England by an unidentified contemporary of Mr. Bastiat, was of much value as a check against this translation. In addition, Dean Russell had his work reviewed by Bertrand de Jouvenel (1903–1987), the noted French economist, historian, and author who was also thoroughly familiar with the English language. Mr. de Jouvenel offered many valuable corrections and suggestions.

The parenthetical expressions and the italicized words throughout this book were supplied by Mr. Bastiat. All subheads and bracketed material were supplied by the translator.

Two of Bastiat's Gems of Economic Reasoning

Daniel J. Sanchez

Now that you have read *The Law*, Frédéric Bastiat's masterpiece of political philosophy, take a few minutes to sample his masterful economics writing.

The next section is an excerpt from his classic 1850 pamphlet, "What Is Seen and What Is Not Seen." (To read the whole thing, visit FEE.org/Bastiat.) Here, Bastiat explains the way of thinking that sets a good economist apart from a bad one. In evaluating an act or policy, the bad economist considers only direct, narrow, and short-term results ("what is seen"), while the good economist also factors in indirect, wider, and longer-term consequences ("what is not seen"). A century later, Henry Hazlitt adopted this as the chief takeaway in his classic 1946 book *Economics in One Lesson*.

Bastiat then applies this general lesson to a specific question in his famous parable of the broken window. Does an act of destruction

---

Daniel J. Sanchez is the Director of Content at the Foundation for Economic Education (FEE) and the editor-in-chief of FEE.org.

actually help the economy by boosting demand for repair services? Many modern-day pundits think so; they see economic silver linings in hurricanes, wars, and other disasters. Bastiat makes plain the fallacy of that line of reasoning in this classic passage.

While backward economic thinking leads some to praise destruction, it leads others to celebrate deprivation. Protectionists, from Bastiat's day to ours, seek to deprive their fellow citizens of foreign goods with trade barriers. Restricting imports, they argue, will increase demand for domestic products, help domestic producers, and so boost the national economy.

In his "A Petition," a satirical 1845 open letter, Bastiat lampoons this illogic with a brilliant *reductio ad absurdum*. Bastiat has the illumination industry of France ask Parliament: why stop at blocking the benefits of foreign merchandise? Using the same logic, why not cover all the windows in the land to block out the benefits of the sun: that ruthless, foreign competitor who unfairly supplies its light for free?

Think of the stimulus to those in the candle business when people must light their dwellings all day long! And to make more candles, there will be a need for more tallow (a substance made from animal fat), so that industry would gain as well. Making more tallow will require more cattle and sheep, so agriculture would boom. The industrial stimulus would go on and on!

Obviously no reasonable person would really believe we can enrich ourselves by blocking out the sun. But it is essentially just as fallacious to think we can enrich ourselves by shutting out the benefits of imports.

For more economics education from Frédéric Bastiat and those who follow in his giant footsteps, visit FEE.org.

The Broken Window

Excerpted from
"What Is Seen and What Is Not Seen"

Introduction

In the economic sphere an act, a habit, an institution, a law produces not only one effect, but a series of effects. Of these effects, the first alone is immediate; it appears simultaneously with its cause; *it is seen*. The other effects emerge only subsequently; *they are not seen*; we are fortunate if we *foresee* them.

There is only one difference between a bad economist and a good one: the bad economist confines himself to the *visible* effect; the good economist takes into account both the effect that can be seen and those effects that must be *foreseen*.

Yet this difference is tremendous; for it almost always happens that when the immediate consequence is favorable, the later consequences are disastrous, and vice versa. Whence it follows that the bad economist pursues a small present good that will be followed by a great evil to come, while the good economist pursues a great good to come, at the risk of a small present evil.

The same thing, of course, is true of health and morals. Often, the sweeter the first fruit of a habit, the more bitter are its later fruits: for example, debauchery, sloth, prodigality. When a man is impressed by the effect *that is seen* and has not yet learned to discern the effects *that are not seen,* he indulges in deplorable habits, not only through natural inclination, but deliberately.

This explains man's necessarily painful evolution. Ignorance surrounds him at his cradle; therefore, he regulates his acts according to their first consequences, the only ones that, in his infancy, he can see. It is only after a long time that he learns to take account of the others. Two very different masters teach him this lesson: experience and foresight. Experience teaches efficaciously but brutally. It instructs us in all the effects of an act by making us feel them, and we cannot fail to learn eventually, from having been burned ourselves, that fire burns. I should prefer, in so far as possible, to replace this rude teacher with one more gentle: foresight. For that reason I shall investigate the consequences of several economic phenomena, contrasting those *that are seen* with those *that are not seen.*

The Broken Window

Have you ever been witness to the fury of that solid citizen, James Goodfellow,[1] when his incorrigible son has happened to break a pane of glass? If you have been present at this spectacle, certainly you must also have observed that the onlookers, even if there are as many as thirty of them, seem with one accord to offer the unfortunate owner the self-same consolation: "It's an ill wind that blows nobody some good. Such accidents keep industry going. Everybody has to make a living. What would become of the glaziers if no one ever broke a window?"

Now, this formula of condolence contains a whole theory that it is a good idea for us to expose, *flagrante delicto,* in this very simple case, since it is exactly the same as that which, unfortunately, underlies most of our economic institutions.

Suppose that it will cost six francs to repair the damage. If you mean that the accident gives six francs' worth of encouragement to the aforesaid industry, I agree. I do not contest it in any way; your reasoning is correct. The glazier will come, do his job, receive six francs, congratulate himself, and bless in his heart the careless child. *That is what is seen.*

But if, by way of deduction, you conclude, as happens only too often, that it is good to break windows, that it helps to circulate money, that it results in encouraging industry in general, I am obliged to cry out: That will never do! Your theory stops at *what is seen*. It does not take account of *what is not seen*.

It is not seen that, since our citizen has spent six francs for one thing, he will not be able to spend them for another. *It is not seen* that if he had not had a windowpane to replace, he would have replaced, for example, his worn-out shoes or added another book to his library. In brief, he would have put his six francs to some use or other for which he will not now have them.

Let us next consider industry *in general*. The window having been broken, the glass industry gets six francs' worth of encouragement; *that is what is seen.*

If the window had not been broken, the shoe industry (or some other) would have received six francs' worth of encouragement; *that is what is not seen.*

And if we were to take into consideration *what is not seen*, because it is a negative factor, as well as *what is seen*, because it is a positive factor, we should understand that there is no benefit to industry *in general* or to *national employment* as a whole, whether windows are broken or not broken.

Now let us consider James Goodfellow.

On the first hypothesis, that of the broken window, he spends six francs and has, neither more nor less than before, the enjoyment of one window.

On the second, that in which the accident did not happen, he would have spent six francs for new shoes and would have had the enjoyment of a pair of shoes as well as of a window.

Now, if James Goodfellow is part of society, we must conclude that society, considering its labors and its enjoyments, has lost the value of the broken window.

From which, by generalizing, we arrive at this unexpected conclusion: "Society loses the value of objects unnecessarily destroyed," and at this aphorism, which will make the hair of the protectionists stand on end: "To break, to destroy, to dissipate is not to encourage national employment," or more briefly: "Destruction is not profitable."

What will the *Moniteur industriel*[2] say to this, or the disciples of the estimable M. de Saint-Chamans,[3] who has calculated with such precision what industry would gain from the burning of Paris, because of the houses that would have to be rebuilt?

I am sorry to upset his ingenious calculations, especially since their spirit has passed into our legislation. But I beg him to begin them again, entering *what is not seen* in the ledger beside *what is seen*.

The reader must apply himself to observe that there are not only two people, but three, in the little drama that I have presented. The one, James Goodfellow, represents the consumer, reduced by destruction to one enjoyment instead of two. The other, under the figure of the glazier, shows us the producer whose industry the accident encourages. The third is the shoemaker (or any other manufacturer) whose industry is correspondingly discouraged by the same cause. It is this third person who is always in the shadow, and who, personifying *what is not seen*, is an essential element of the problem. It is he who makes us understand how absurd it is to see a profit in destruction. It is he who will soon teach us that it is equally absurd to see a profit in trade restriction, which is, after all, nothing more nor less than partial destruction. So, if you get to the bottom of all the arguments advanced in favor of restrictionist measures, you will find only a paraphrase of that common cliché: *"What would become of the glaziers if no one ever broke any windows?"*

1. In French, *Jacques Bonhomme*, used like "John Bull" in English to represent the practical, responsible, unassuming average man.—Translator.

2. Newspaper of the Committee for the Defense of Domestic Industry, a protectionist organization.—Translator.

3. Auguste, Vicomte de Saint-Chamans (1777–1861), Deputy and Councillor of State under the Restoration, protectionist and upholder of the balance of trade. His celebrated stand on the "obstacle" here quoted by Bastiat comes from his *Nouvel essai sur la richesse des nations*, 1824. This work was later (1852) incorporated in his *Traité d'économie politique*.—Translator.

The Candlemakers' Petition

Originally published as "A Petition."

From the Manufacturers of Candles, Tapers, Lanterns, Candlesticks, Street Lamps, Snuffers, and Extinguishers, and from the Producers of Tallow, Oil, Resin, Alcohol, and Generally of Everything Connected with Lighting.

To the Honorable Members of the Chamber of Deputies.

Gentlemen:

You are on the right track. You reject abstract theories and have little regard for abundance and low prices. You concern yourselves mainly with the fate of the producer. You wish to free him from foreign competition, that is, to reserve the *domestic market* for *domestic industry.*

We come to offer you a wonderful opportunity for applying your—what shall we call it? Your theory? No, nothing is more deceptive than theory. Your doctrine? Your system? Your principle? But you dislike doctrines, you have a horror of systems, and, as for principles, you deny that there are any in political economy; therefore we shall call it your practice—your practice without theory and without principle.

We are suffering from the ruinous competition of a foreign rival who apparently works under conditions so far superior to our own for the production of light that he is *flooding* the *domestic market* with it at an incredibly low price; for the moment he appears, our sales cease, all the consumers turn to him, and a branch of French industry whose ramifications are innumerable is all at once reduced to complete stagnation. This rival, which is none other than the sun, is waging war on us so mercilessly that we suspect he is being stirred up against us by perfidious Albion (excellent diplomacy nowadays!), particularly because he has for that haughty island a respect that he does not show for us.★

We ask you to be so good as to pass a law requiring the closing of all windows, dormers, skylights, inside and outside shutters, curtains, casements, bull's-eyes, deadlights, and blinds—in short, all openings, holes, chinks, and fissures through which the light of the sun is wont to enter houses, to the detriment of the fair industries with which, we are proud to say, we have endowed the country, a country that cannot, without betraying ingratitude, abandon us today to so unequal a combat.

Be good enough, honorable deputies, to take our request seriously, and do not reject it without at least hearing the reasons that we have to advance in its support.

First, if you shut off as much as possible all access to natural light, and thereby create a need for artificial light, what industry in France will not ultimately be encouraged?

If France consumes more tallow, there will have to be more cattle and sheep, and, consequently, we shall see an increase in cleared fields, meat, wool, leather, and especially manure, the basis of all agricultural wealth.

If France consumes more oil, we shall see an expansion in the cultivation of the poppy, the olive, and rapeseed. These rich yet soil-exhausting plants will come at just the right time to enable us to put to profitable use the increased fertility that the breeding of cattle will impart to the land.

Our moors will be covered with resinous trees. Numerous

★Translator's note: "Perfidious Albion" is England, along with a typically French jibe at the English fog, which keeps the sun from interfering with artificial light in England as much as it does in France. During the 1840's, Franco-English relations were occasionally very tense.

swarms of bees will gather from our mountains the perfumed trea-
sures that today waste their fragrance, like the flowers from which they
emanate. Thus, there is not one branch of agriculture that would not
undergo a great expansion.

The same holds true of shipping. Thousands of vessels will engage
in whaling, and in a short time we shall have a fleet capable of uphold-
ing the honor of France and of gratifying the patriotic aspirations of
the undersigned petitioners, chandlers, etc.

But what shall we say of the *specialties of Parisian manufacture*?
Henceforth you will behold gilding, bronze, and crystal in candlesticks,
in lamps, in chandeliers, in candelabra sparkling in spacious emporia
compared with which those of today are but stalls.

There is no needy resin-collector on the heights of his sand
dunes, no poor miner in the depths of his black pit, who will not
receive higher wages and enjoy increased prosperity.

It needs but a little reflection, gentlemen, to be convinced that
there is perhaps not one Frenchman, from the wealthy stockholder of
the Anzin Company to the humblest vendor of matches, whose condition would not be improved by the success of our petition.

We anticipate your objections, gentlemen; but there is not a single
one of them that you have not picked up from the musty old books
of the advocates of free trade. We defy you to utter a word against us
that will not instantly rebound against yourselves and the principle that
guides your entire policy.

Will you tell us that, though we may gain by this protection,
France will not gain at all, because the consumer will bear the expense?

We have our answer ready:

You no longer have the right to invoke the interests of the consumer. You have sacrificed him whenever you have found his interests
opposed to those of the producer. You have done so in order *to encourage industry and to increase employment*. For the same reason you
ought to do so this time too.

Indeed, you yourselves have anticipated this objection. When told that the consumer has a stake in the free entry of iron, coal, sesame, wheat, and textiles, "Yes," you reply, "but the producer has a stake in their exclusion." Very well, surely if consumers have a stake in the admission of natural light, producers have a stake in its interdiction.

"But," you may still say, "the producer and the consumer are one and the same person. If the manufacturer profits by protection, he will make the farmer prosperous. Contrariwise, if agriculture is prosperous, it will open markets for manufactured goods." Very well! If you grant us a monopoly over the production of lighting during the day, first of all we shall buy large amounts of tallow, charcoal, oil, resin, wax, alcohol, silver, iron, bronze, and crystal, to supply our industry; and, moreover, we and our numerous suppliers, having become rich, will consume a great deal and spread prosperity into all areas of domestic industry.

Will you say that the light of the sun is a gratuitous gift of Nature, and that to reject such gifts would be to reject wealth itself under the pretext of encouraging the means of acquiring it?

But if you take this position, you strike a mortal blow at your own policy; remember that up to now you have always excluded foreign goods *because* and *in proportion as* they approximate gratuitous gifts. You have only *half* as good a reason for complying with the demands of other monopolists as you have for granting our petition, which is in *complete* accord with your established policy; and to reject our demands precisely because they are *better founded* than anyone else's would be tantamount to accepting the equation: $+ \times + = -$; in other words, it would be to heap *absurdity* upon *absurdity*.

Labor and Nature collaborate in varying proportions, depending upon the country and the climate, in the production of a commodity. The part that Nature contributes is always free of charge; it is the part contributed by human labor that constitutes value and is paid for.

If an orange from Lisbon sells for half the price of an orange from Paris, it is because the natural heat of the sun, which is, of course, free of charge, does for the former what the latter owes to artificial heating, which necessarily has to be paid for in the market.

Thus, when an orange reaches us from Portugal, one can say that it is given to us half free of charge, or, in other words, at *half price* as compared with those from Paris.

Now, it is precisely on the basis of its being *semigratuitous* (pardon the word) that you maintain it should be barred. You ask: "How can French labor withstand the competition of foreign labor when the former has to do all the work, whereas the latter has to do only half, the sun taking care of the rest?" But if the fact that a product is *half* free of charge leads you to exclude it from competition, how can its being *totally* free of charge induce you to admit it into competition? Either you are not consistent, or you should, after excluding what is half free of charge as harmful to our domestic industry, exclude what is totally gratuitous with all the more reason and with twice the zeal.

To take another example: When a product—coal, iron, wheat, or textiles—comes to us from abroad, and when we can acquire it for less labor than if we produced it ourselves, the difference is a *gratuitous gift* that is conferred upon us. The size of this gift is proportionate to the extent of this difference. It is a quarter, a half, or three-quarters of the value of the product if the foreigner asks of us only three-quarters, one-half, or one-quarter as high a price. It is as complete as it can be when the donor, like the sun in providing us with light, asks nothing from us. The question, and we pose it formally, is whether what you desire for France is the benefit of consumption free of charge or the alleged advantages of onerous production. Make your choice, but be logical; for as long as you ban, as you do, foreign coal, iron, wheat, and textiles, *in proportion* as their price approaches *zero,* how inconsistent it would be to admit the light of the sun, whose price is zero all day long!

The Wisdom
of
Frédéric Bastiat

Politics

I cannot legitimately force my fellow men to be industrious, sober, thrifty, generous, learned, or pious; but I can force them to be just.

For the same reason, the collective force cannot be legitimately employed to foster the love of labor, sobriety, thrift, generosity, learning, religious faith; but it can be legitimately employed to further the rule of justice, to defend every man's rights.

Try to imagine a system of labor imposed by force that is not a violation of liberty; a transfer of wealth imposed by force that is not a violation of property rights. If you cannot do so, then you must agree that the law cannot organize labor and industry without organizing injustice.

Unhappy country, where the sacred forces that were meant to support each man's rights are perverted to accomplish themselves the violation of these rights.

Shall I speak of the corrupting immorality that seeps into the veins of the whole body politic when, in principle, the law puts itself at the service of every spoliative impulse? Attend a meeting of the National Assembly when bonuses, subsidies, bounties, restrictions are on the agenda. See with what shameless rapacity everyone tries to make sure of his share of the plunder—plunder to which he would blush to stoop as a private individual.

How could men dream of blaming themselves for their woes when they have been persuaded that by nature they are inert, that the source of all action, and consequently of all responsibility, lies outside themselves, in the will of the sovereign and of the lawgiver?

Certain nations seem particularly liable to fall prey to governmental plunder. They are those in which men, lacking faith in their own dignity and capability, would feel themselves lost if they were not *governed and administered* every step of the way.... I have seen countries in which the people think that agriculture can make no progress unless the government supports experimental farms; that soon there will no longer be any horses, if the government does not provide studs; that fathers will not have their children educated, or will have them taught only immorality, if the government does not decide what it is proper to learn.

People are beginning to realize that the apparatus of government is costly. But what they do not know is that the burden falls *inevitably* on them.

&

When a nation is burdened with taxes, nothing is more difficult, as I would say, impossible, than to levy them equally. The statisticians and fiscal authorities no longer even try to do so. What is still more difficult, however, is to shift the tax burden onto the shoulders of the rich. The state can have an abundance of money only by taking from everyone and especially from the masses.

&

In a country where no law may be voted and no tax may be levied save with the consent of those whom the law is to govern and upon whom the tax is to fall, the public can be robbed only if it is first deceived. Our ignorance is the *raw material* of every extortion that is practiced upon us, and we may be certain beforehand that every sophism is the precursor of an act of plunder. My friends, when you detect a sophism in a petition, get a good grip on your wallet, for you may be sure that this is what the petitioners are aiming at.

&

In the realm of government operation it may happen that functionaries receive services from the citizens without rendering services in return; in that case the taxpayer suffers a loss, no matter what illusion the circulation of bank notes may create.

…the state has no resources of its own. It has nothing, it possesses nothing that it does not take from the workers. When, then, it meddles in everything, it substitutes the deplorable and costly activity of its own agents for private activity.

…we must wait until we have learned by experience—perhaps cruel experience—to trust in the state a little less and in mankind a little more.

…the government offers to cure all the ills of mankind. It promises to restore commerce, make agriculture prosperous, expand industry, encourage arts and letters, wipe out poverty, etc., etc. All that is needed is to create some new government agencies and to pay a few more bureaucrats.

The state too is subject to the Malthusian law. It tends to expand in proportion to its means of existence and to live beyond its means, and these are, in the last analysis, nothing but the substance of the people.

Economics

"In the sweat of thy face shalt thou eat bread." But everyone wants as much bread and as little sweat as possible.

…certain men have recourse to the law in order to abridge the natural prerogatives of this freedom on the part of other men. This kind of plunder is called privilege or monopoly.

This is called …brotherhood: "You have produced; I have not; we are comrades; let us share." "You own something; I own nothing; we are brothers; let us share."

𝒫

Let a merchant begin to sell his good on the principle of brotherly love, and I do not give him even a month before his children will be reduced to beggary.

𝒫

It is indeed a singular thing that people wish to pass laws to nullify the disagreeable consequences that the law of responsibility entails. Will they never realize that they do not eliminate these consequences, but merely pass them along to other people? The result is one injustice the more and one moral lesson the less....

𝒫

The poorest class in civilized countries is far above the poorest class among savage peoples. It has risen so far; why should it not rise even higher?

𝒫

The present level of consumption enjoyed by an honest and industrious working-class family does not surprise us because habit has familiarized us with this strange situation. If, however, we were to compare the standard of living that this family has attained with the one that would be its lot in a hypothetical social order from which competition had been excluded; …we should realize that freedom, despite all still-existing restrictions on it, has wrought a miracle so enduring that for that very reason we fail to be aware of it.

We are endowed with the faculty of comparing, of judging, of choosing, and of acting accordingly. This implies that we can arrive at a good or a bad judgment, make a good or a bad choice—a fact that it is never idle to remind men of when we speak to them of liberty.

...is it so difficult to permit men to experiment, to feel their way, to choose, to make mistakes, to correct them, to learn, to work together, to manage their own property and their own interests, to act for themselves, at their own risk and peril, on their own responsibility?

Do we not see that this is what makes them men? Must we always start with the fatal premise that all those who govern are guardians and all the governed are wards?

For my part, it seems to me that there is a connection between the aspiration that impels all men toward the improvement of their material, intellectual, and moral condition, and the faculties with which they are endowed to realize this aspiration.

Hence, I should like each man to have, on his own responsibility, the free disposition, administration, and control of his own person, his acts, his family, his transactions, his associations, his intelligence, his faculties, his labor, his capital, and his property.

Advise me, but do not force your opinion on me. I shall decide at my *peril and risk*; that is enough, and for the law to interfere would be tyranny.

...since liberty is still a sacred word and still has the power to stir men's hearts, her enemies would strip her of her name and her prestige and, rechristening her *competition*, would lead her forth to sacrifice while the applauding multitudes extend their hands to receive their chains of slavery.

Competition is merely the absence of oppression.

...self-interest is that indomitable individualistic force within us that urges us on to progress and discovery, but at the same time disposes us to monopolize our discoveries. Competition is that no less indomitable humanitarian force that wrests progress, as fast as it is made, from the hands of the individual and places it at the disposal of all mankind. These two forces, which may well be deplored when considered individually, work together to create our social harmony.

By virtue of exchange, one man's prosperity is beneficial to all others.

...if coercion assumes endless forms, freedom has only one. Once again, the free and voluntary transfer of services from one person to another can be defined in these simple words: "Give me this, and I will give you that. Do this for me, and I will do that for you."

In a country like the United States, where the right to property is placed above the law, where the sole function of the public police force is to safeguard this natural right, each person can in full confidence dedicate his capital and his labor to production. He does not have to fear that his plans and calculations will be upset from one instant to another by the legislature.

Social Engineers

...one of the saddest sights that can present itself to anyone who loves mankind is that of a productive age bending all its efforts to infect itself—by way of education—with the thoughts, the sentiments, the errors, the prejudices, and the vices of a nation of plunderers. Our age is often accused of a lack of consistency, of a failure to show any correlation between the ideals it professes and the way of life it pursues. The criticism is just, and I believe that I have here indicated the principal reason why this situation prevails.

It is the unfortunate obsession of our age to wish to give pure abstractions a life of their own, to imagine a city apart from the people who live in it, mankind independently of the individual men who constitute it, a whole aside from its component parts, collective life without the individual units that comprise it.

Can the human race establish a new basis for property, family, labor, and exchange every day in the year? Can it risk changing the social order every morning?

There are too many "great" men in the world; there are too many legislators, planners, founders of societies, leaders of nations, fathers of their country, etc., etc. Too many people place themselves above mankind in order to guide its footsteps; too many people make a career of being concerned with mankind.

As we have seen, the legislator, according to the ideas of the ancients, bears the same relation to mankind as the potter does to the clay. Unfortunately, when this idea prevails, nobody wants to be the clay, and everyone wants to be the potter.

I confess that I am one of those who think that the choice, the impulse, should come from below, not from above, from the citizens, not from the legislator; and the contrary doctrine seems to me to lead to the annihilation of liberty and of human dignity.

…when the law, by the intervention of its necessary agent, force, imposes a system of labor, a method or a subject of education, a faith or a religion, its action on men is no longer negative, but positive. It substitutes the will of the legislator for their own will, the initiative of the legislator for their own initiative.

They no longer have to take counsel together, to compare, to foresee; the law does all this for them. Intelligence becomes a useless accessory; they cease to be men; they lose their personality, their liberty, their property.

Let us, therefore, not have the presumption to overthrow everything, to regulate everything, to seek to exempt all, men and things alike, from the operation of the laws to which they are naturally subject.... Let us not make ourselves ridiculous by proposing to change humanity, as if we stood apart from it and from its errors and shortcomings.

If by ill-advised measures you free men from the responsibility of their acts, they could still be taught by theory—but no longer by experience. And I am not certain that instruction that is not reinforced and backed by experience is not more dangerous than ignorance itself.

Meanwhile, socialism has carried its folly so far as to announce the end of all the ills of society, though not of all the ills of the individual. It has not yet dared to predict that man will reach the point where suffering, old age, and death will be eliminated.

The admirers of unity are very numerous, and that is understandable. By a providential decree, we all have faith in our own judgment, and we believe that there is only one right opinion in the world, namely, our own. Therefore we think that the legislator could do no better than to impose it on everyone; and, the better to be on the safe side, we all want to be that legislator.

But once the legislator is elected and freed from his campaign promises, oh, then his language changes! The nation returns to passivity, to inertia, to nothingness, and the legislator takes on the character of omnipotence. His the invention, his the direction, his the impulsion, his the organization. Mankind has nothing to do but to let things be done to it; the hour of despotism has arrived.

For what precise and definite object are all the citizens today to be stamped, like the coinage, with the same image? ...On what basis would they be cast in the same mold? *And who will possess the mold?* A terrible question, which should give us pause. *Who will possess the mold?*

Property is a necessary consequence of the nature of man.

In the full sense of the word, *man is born a proprietor,* because he is born with wants whose satisfaction is necessary to life, and with organs and faculties whose exercise is indispensable to the satisfaction of these wants. Faculties are only the extension of the person; and property is nothing but an extension of the faculties...

To tamper with man's freedom is not only to injure him, to degrade him; it is to change his nature, to render him, insofar as such oppression is exercised, incapable of improvement; it is to strip him of his resemblance to the Creator, to stifle within him the noble breath of life with which he was endowed at his creation.

The Future

Every attempt to divert responsibility from its natural course is an attack upon justice, freedom, order, civilization, or progress.

...gentlemen, organize industry as much as you please. But we, for our part, will take care to see that you do not organize *robbery*.

It is not, as people think, the monopolists, but the monopolized, that sustain the monopolies.

When misguided public opinion honors what is despicable and despises what is honorable, punishes virtue and rewards vice, encourages what is harmful and discourages what is useful, applauds falsehood and smothers truth under indifference or insult, a nation turns its back on progress and can be restored only by the terrible lessons of catastrophe.

When education has sown a fatal seed in the soil of public opinion, there is in the body politic a force of self-preservation, *vis medicatrix,* that enables it to rid itself, at long last, after many sufferings and tears, of the baneful germ with which it has become infected.

What is freedom? It is the sum total of all our freedoms. To be free, on one's own responsibility, to think and to act, to speak and to write, to labor and to exchange, to teach and to learn—this alone is to be free.

I have not made an alliance with anyone; I have not joined either side. On each question, I have voted according to my own conscience.

WE INVITE YOU TO ADVANCE LIBERTY WITH US.